CREATE A
Polymer Clay
IMPRESSION

Sarajane Helm

Published by

**krause
publications**

700 East State Street • Iola, WI 54990-0001
715/445-2214 • FAX: 715/445-4087   www.krause.com

Please call or write for our free catalog of publications. Our toll-free number to place an order or
obtain a free catalog is 800-258-0929 or please use our regular business telephone 715-445-2214.

Library of Congress Catalog Number 2001090486
ISBN 0-87341-988-X

Acknowledgment

Our heartfelt thanks and appreciation go to all the family, friends, teachers, librarians, students, patrons, landlords, editors, co-workers, critics and other sources of inspiration in our lives. Without their support, patience, and influence this book would not have happened.

Foreword

In 1989 I was exposed to the wonderful material that is the subject of this book. It was a little strange; a plastic clay, colorful with brilliant hues, soft and malleable, and hardened in an oven! Wow! It could be used in so many different ways and I had never even heard of it before. Where on earth had this wonderful stuff been hiding? At the time, I was interested in the beautiful old glass millefiori beads from Venice and was passionately in love with ancient Roman glass mosaic pieces that were on display in Washington, D.C.'s Freer Gallery of Art. As I was being shown how to make my own millefiori designs by Kathleen Dustin, in a fateful class at The Torpedo Factory Art Center, the connections were exploding in my head. I don't think I slept for several days after that class, I was so excited! The 60 or so of us that attended that incredible class lost our composure that day.

It was the beginning of a movement. Through an accident of fate, I was asked to write a book about the material, the first book that pulled together all the diverse information on the clay that came to be called polymer clay.

In 1991, *The New Clay* was published. It was a wonderful collaboration of all the artists across the country that were familiar with and developing new ways to work with the clay. A little knowledge can have a powerful effect. The simple act of compiling the information in one place fanned the flames of curiosity and soon artists all across the country were creating and teaching with polymer clay. A national guild was founded in Washington, D.C. In the 10 or so years that have passed, the movement has grown exponentially and continues to grow today.

The clay is fun, easy to work with, uses only simple tools or none at all, and is a chameleon for new techniques and those borrowed from other art and craft disciplines. This is one of the few really new materials to arise in a long, long time. Born in the 20th century with few preconceived traditions associated with it, the clay is wide open to all uses and techniques.

Everyone seems to be seduced by it and I am sure you will be, too. Enjoy exploring this wonderful material with Sarajane's book. It is the latest of a growing number of exciting books that are teaching and spreading the word about polymer clay and the polymer clay movement that is taking the country by storm.

May your own personal muses be unleashed by your experiences with this magical stuff. Enjoy!

Yours, Nan Roche

Contents

Create a Polymer Clay Impression

*F*unk and Wagnall's Standard Dictionary defines "poly-" as "many; several; much" and it certainly holds true in the case of polymer clays. The chemical components themselves are formed of long chains of molecules, and there is also a mental and social aspect that shows this definition to be true—not only are artists able to string together their learned abilities and use them with polymer clay, but the artists themselves are often found linking together to form a stronger bond. Over and over I have heard people say how very supportive and sharing polymer clay artists are, and the common fund of knowledge, tips and techniques develops and grows in unexpected ways due to this flow of ideas and observed results.

Synchronicity happens when many people "discover" the same ideas at the same time. I personally know many people who recognized independently that pasta rollers would make great polymer clay tools. What is even more interesting to me is the way three artists can take the very same information and follow three distinctly different trails of discovery, finding ways to realize their artistic vision that are deeply personal and unique. This is true even while they work with the same medium!

Polymer clays are one of the most exciting and versatile developments in the world of art supplies. When used according to the package directions, these clays, (which are sold under brand names like FIMO™, Cernit™, Sculpey™ and Premo™, to name just a few) are easy and safe to use at home. Unlike earth clays, polymer clays do not mix with water and so do not dry out, though they will degrade over time without proper storage. They don't require expensive tools and equipment, such as a kiln. They are available widely through craft stores, art supply stores, fabric supply stores, and through mail order. Many companies now sell supplies via the Internet. Never before has such a wide variety of high-quality art material been available to so many people, with such a wide variety of backgrounds and talents in making and decorating. Is it any wonder there is a giant explosion of interest right now in learning creative skills and using the ones already known in new ways?

Polymer clay is an artist's dream medium in that in becomes whatever you want it to be, much like the "Shmoo" creatures in "Li'l Abner." You can model it, sculpt it, cast it, cane it, paint it, animate it, and I'm told that some people can even throw it on a wheel.

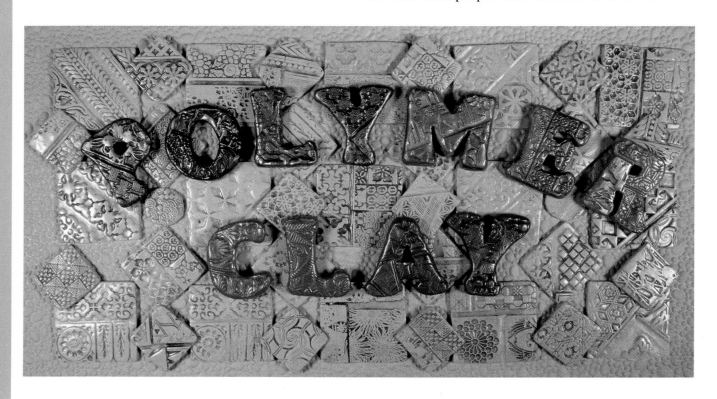

You can wear it or decorate with it. It can be made to look like bone or semi-precious stone, coral or shell, like leather or lace, and all sorts of fabric in between. It can mimic wood or metal, and can be used to model the features of a realistic sleeping baby, or a warrior elf.

You can play with it. You can work with it. You can make stuff with it.

Everyone—regardless of skill level—can have a fun and gratifying experience with polymer clay. Of course, there are a few things you can do to ensure this—buy fresh clay, and store it properly. Condition even soft clays thoroughly and bake all clays according to directions. Most breakage is the direct result of incomplete conditioning or under baking.

After more than a decade of seeing what all I can do with polymer clays, I still find new things all the time. Polymer clay artists share information quite freely, and there are many fine teachers available both in person, and through books and videos, magazines, Internet news-groups and Web sites. I've learned a great deal by looking at what other professional artists can do with polymer clay, and by looking at what my students and my children do with it. Most of what I've learned has come from exposure to the stuff itself, as we all really learn best by doing.

Some of the most valuable lessons have come from things I attempted that didn't come off the way I planned. (Some think of these as mistakes, but they really aren't.) Another way to learn more is to just "mess around" and have a play day, where no production work or planned projects are allowed. If you have trouble allowing yourself unstructured creative time, invite a few friends. This makes it "official" and helps get the time censors we all face to approve some time to experiment and push the boundaries of what we already know. In most cases, hobby/craft knowledge (and tools) from one area such as quilting, rubber stamping, miniature or model making can be cross-utilized with polymer clays.

One of the most seductive aspects of polymer clay work is that the wide array of colors already available can be mixed to any desired shade, tone, or hue. Fabrics can be matched for use in decorative items for the home or for wearable art. With textural and color coordination, you can make just about anything "go with" or match within your chosen design plan. It is a pure delight for the costume designer or doll maker, as accessories such as crowns, scepters, period buttons and even masks or armor pieces are easily fabricated.

Part I
Fundamentals

Preparation

Whatever you decide to make, polymer clays, like earth clays, must first be prepared by kneading and rolling. Clay will pick up any dirt or natural oils—this is especially apparent with white and light colors. Baby towelettes work very well for polymer clean-up jobs, and don't dry your hands out too badly. Beware of clothing with loose fibers such as knits. My favorite black sweater is now banned from the studio due to the little bits of it I found in the clay every time I wore it to work. Clean your work surface too, and be aware that raw clays will dull or even remove finishes from a wood surface.

Tile, glass, marble, acrylic sheets, Formica™, Melamine™ or Masonite™ pieces make good portable work areas, with the smooth surfaces making each easy to use and clean. Most of these are available at hardware stores, where some are sold as shelving. Ceramic and stone tiles meant for floors are also good work surfaces. They stay cool and are easily cleaned.

Marble slabs meant for candy making are another option. Banquet tables make a very strong work table and have the added benefit of being sturdy enough to hold the clamp of a pasta roller. Acrylic sheets and acrylic rods for rolling the clay can be found at shops that fabricate signs for businesses. Look in your Yellow Pages under "plastics," "acrylics" or "signs".

If your clay is very hard, you can soften it by using a food processor with the chopping blade reserved for clay only. A few drops of vegetable oil can be added while using the processor. Do not pour from the bottle, as this is hard to control. Instead, pour a few drops into the cap or a spoon and add from there. Run the food processor in short bursts, and don't leave it unattended, as the clay will heat during use. This is helpful in small doses, but you don't want it to overheat. It can start to cook if left too long. Clays that have already been conditioned can be re-chopped to achieve very realistic mottled stone effects.

To add small amounts of oil by hand, coat your hands lightly and continue to work the clay. Or, you can add transparent clay, which is softer and adds plasticiser to hard clays. There's a product on the market called "Mix Quick™" that is very helpful for softening hard clay. It contains even more of the plasticiser than the translucent clay. If your clay is like a rock, try processing it with any of these, and then put it in a plastic sandwich bag or wrap the resulting lump with plastic wrap and leave it overnight. This allows the active ingredients to "travel" and helps to permeate the old clay with new plasticiser. Then flatten the clay and condition as usual. It takes a little extra effort, but most old clays can be revitalized in this manner.

If the clay is not just old, but partially baked, it may not be possible to re-soften it. On the rare occasion that this happens, I chop the clay using the food processor and use the bits as rock-like inclusions if the color is appropriate—if not, I add a little gold, silver or copper powder to the chopped bits in the bowl of the processor, and whirl it again. I pour the resulting "nuggets" onto a baking pan, spread lightly, then bake. These can be used as inclusions in soft clay, or can be glued into place as is. They look just like raw metal nuggets. You can also make miniature rocks and pebbles in this fashion (leaving out the metal powders) that can be wonderfully useful with miniature displays.

If your clays are too soft, they can be made more workable by "wicking" or "leaching" the excess plasticiser from the clay. To do this, roll the clay into sheets and place it between two pieces of paper. The oily film that soaks into the paper is the plasticiser, a chemical solvent, and should be disposed of safely in the trash. Different consistencies of clay can also be mixed to

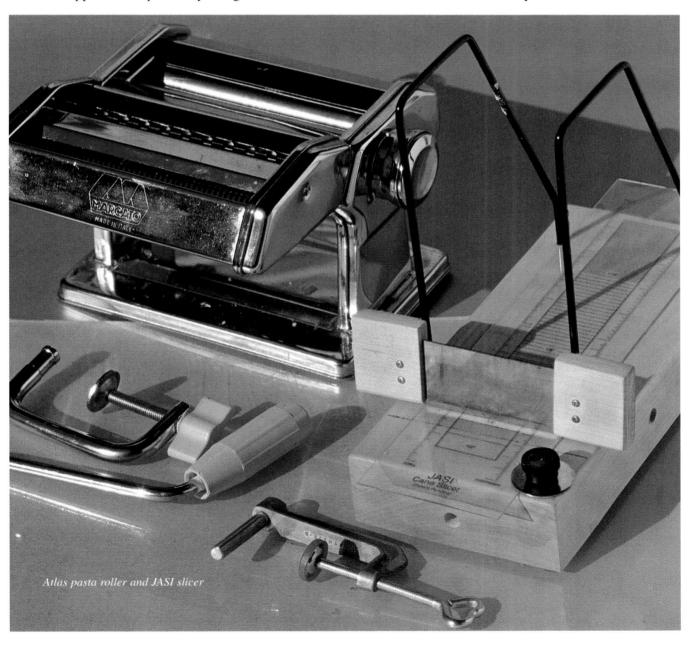

Atlas pasta roller and JASI slicer

pearlescent palette

cool palette

warm palette

neutral palette

find a happier medium. When mixing old, hard clay and new, soft clay, a messy sort of shredding takes place. It eventually will all work together, but this can also be used to create very interesting effects as the clay is put through the pasta roller. Sometimes I even do it on purpose.

Use a thin sheet of old clay (leave some out for a week or two uncovered if you don't have any already) and place it on top of a thicker slab of softer clay in a different color, then roll it down to pancake thickness and put it through the pasta roller on the widest setting. As it starts to break up, fold the clay tongue so that an interesting-looking patch is on top, with the rest of the clay padding the underneath. Then put it through the rollers again. It will start to look like watercolor splotches, stone, even tortoiseshell, if done with the right colors. If the sheet is getting too thin, pad it with more clay, or just keep folding what you have, keeping the part you like on top.

This is one of the effects we have stumbled onto by accident, and an example of what we call the "I meant to do that" school of artistic techniques. Many times what seems to be a mistake or problem is actually the start of some new effect. People will ask, "How did you DO that?" and we smile and say, "Oh, it's a special way…we meant to do that!"

For those with wrist or hand strength problems, or who are working with large quantities, a pasta roller can be used to knead the clay. This has the added advantage of rolling the clay into even sheets of adjustable thickness. Color blending is also made faster and easier by using a roller, or is accomplished by hand by rolling and kneading two or more colors of clay until they blend. Partial blending is used for a marbled effect, but individual colors should be conditioned first, as continued kneading will result in a solid color or shade that differs from the original colors.

To condition, slice and chop clay by hand or with a processor. Roll the clay out into a snake shape, then ball it up, and roll it out again. Flatten it into a pancake about 1/2-inch thick or less, and put it through the pasta roller at the widest setting (a #1 on many machines, though some work backwards and start at #7). This produces a sheet or "tongue" of clay. Fold it in half lengthwise, and place the fold side down in the roller or along either side but not on top—the fold on top traps air bubbles. Repeat the process. Do this several times. If the clay crumbles, roll it back into a snake and start over. Some very hard clays benefit from a little pre-warming, and some people wear blocks of clay in their pockets, stuffed in their bras or shirts, or they sit on them. Do be careful to remove all packets before that quick trip to the store, or you risk getting some very strange looks! My husband, Bryan, has bigger, warmer, stronger hands than I do, and has taken over conditioning much of the clay. We go through many pounds at a time. This arrangement has freed me to spend more time on design work. Tip: It is often worth offering incentives to get others involved.

Polymer clays come in so many colors to begin with, and blending offers infinite variety. Colors can often benefit from having a small amount of white added in the conditioning step. The pigment helps keep the color from darkening when baked, which is more of a problem with some colors and clays than others. The more opaque clays do not darken as much as those that have a transparent base. Some clay colors, such as FIMO™ red, purple and navy, also seem to darken more with baking, as do brands with a waxier appearance such as Cernit™. I also add black to much of my clay palette to "sadden" or tone down the intensity of the colors. I prefer muted shades, or vibrant colors that are not necessarily bright, but if you like brights, try adding the florescent colors to your mixes. Violet and florescent pink make the most wonderful purples. Adding small amounts of florescent colors can really perk things up.

Clays can be kneaded and then left to await your convenience. They will not dry out or harden unless they are heated—if they are properly stored. I prepare my clays in quantity, and wrap the large chunks in plastic wrap, and then break off pieces as needed. A quick roll in the hands to warm the clay is usually all that's needed once I'm ready to begin. I also use sheets of plastic wrap to cover work in progress if I need to leave it for any length of time, and to wrap cane lengths.

Not all plastic wraps are compatible with clay, but HandiWrap is. I'm told this product has been bought by the manufacturer of Saran™ products, and is now being repackaged as "Saran™ with Cling." It appears to be compatible. You need to be alert when using new products with clay. If there seems to be any melting over time, then the plasticisers of one are eating the other, and the plastics are not compatible. Once you find something that works, stick with it if you can. Covering with plastic wrap helps keep raw clay soft and workable. I have some canes that are three to six years old that are fine.

Covering works in progress keeps dust, cat hair, and other unwanted bits that are present in the air from settling onto the clay. It is far easier to protect a piece than it is to clean it up afterwards. I also protect my clays from exposure to ultraviolet light by keeping extra canes in a covered box, and by placing cloth covers on the stored bulk clays. A towel or length of fabric works fine for this purpose. Don't keep clay on a windowsill in direct light. The clays begin to cure at temperatures of 110 degrees, so watch where you store them. Don't leave them in the car, or on top of the appliances.

Many other things can also be added to the clays. Dried spices or vegetable matter, pigments and powders can all be worked into the clay. PearlEx™ powders are particularly useful as they are mica based and have a wide range of metallic and reflective colors. FIMO™ Bronzepulver and other metallic powders are made with powdered aluminum, and give the most clearly defined image when stamping, but require more care and caution in use. Make very sure not to breath in these powders. Wear a respirator or filter mask if you work much with these. Even talcum powder, used as a mold release, contains ground rock with a small amount of asbestos, so get in the habit of working with powders in an unhurried manner so as not to produce clouds. If there is a spill, wait until the dust settles, and then clean up with a damp paper towel. I use a scented talcum powder, and if I can smell it I know I am flinging it about too much.

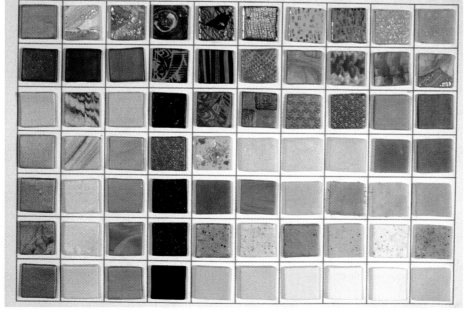

neutral effects sampler

Using a brush to apply powders of any kind seems to be a bad idea, and the glinting dust motes in the air are pretty but undesirable. I apply powders in other ways, lightly using a ponce bag for my talc, and using my index finger to apply metallic powders. I have been assured that the aluminum is too big a molecule to get through the skin. The greater danger from aluminum comes when it is breathed, unless metal allergies are present—then it is a good idea to stay away from the bronzpulvers completely. Always wash hands right away after using the powders so you don't accidentally get it in your eyes or elsewhere. It also keeps the rest of the clay in your studio cleaner. I keep a towelette out to use for this as needed.

Mixing powders directly into the clay can create some very beautiful effects. Stamped pieces that are not quite right can be wadded back up, and the powder dispersed into the clay. The more translucent the clay, the more powders and other inclusions seem to float. Opalescent effects can be brought about, especially when translucent clays are buffed to a high sheen. Glitter, confetti, fibers and more can be used on top, or mixed into, polymer clays. So can some stamp embossing powders, and some dyes. Very fine "microcrystalline" glitter is particularly effective. Metallic foils or leaf can be used to spectacular effect, especially with translucent clays.

Mokume Gane is a technique that uses a lot of metallic foils, and the leftover bits from that process can be used by further working the clay and foils into tiny pieces that are distributed throughout. Nan Roche and Lindly Haunani have both written about this technique and adaptations they have formulated. In effect, layers of translucent or colored clays are built up with metallic leaf sandwiched in between each thin layer. A "loaf" is thus built up of layers, and then the layers are displaced from pressure underneath, using small chunks of clay in some versions or more solid objects (which are removed) in other versions. The loaf is carefully patted and poked and formed down around the displacing items, creating mounds and valleys. The clay can then be sliced very thinly across the top, revealing rings and striations that are quite lovely. These slices can be layered over different colors of base clay. It is important to use a very sharp blade and get very thin slices. Microtomes are blades designed for making biopsy tissue slices and work very well for this. Nu-blades are larger and just as sharp. Use caution with all sharp blades. Buffing can make the baked translucent clay very glassy, and the inclusions seem to float within.

When powders are used in a surface application such as rubber stamping or with exposed foils, a protective covering must be added to the baked clay. Inclusions inside clay are protected by the clay itself, but if cut edges of metal foils are in contact with air and moisture, they can lead to tarnish or patination and staining of the clay long after baking. I have found this to be particularly true with Mokume Gane that has been made with Sculpey clay. It is also more prevalent with metallic composition leaf, as opposed to higher grades of gold and silver. When sealed correctly, however, the less expensive composition leaf is very suitable for polymer clay and retains its beauty for years.

Aluminum leaf can be used in place of silver because the color is the same, and gold composition leaf is much less expensive than 22-karat gold leaf. Copper is also available, and so are many "colored" types. Accent Imports and Exports has a line called "magic leaf" that has patterns of color on the leaf—stars, stripes, squares and more. Even when broken apart on polymer clay these give a swath of sparkle and color, and when used as a solid covering it is splendid.

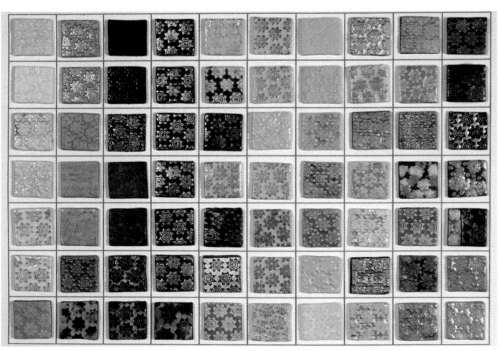

neutral stamp sampler

Finishes

After years of research, the best product I have found for use as a finish on polymer clay is available at most hardware stores. The full name is Flecto Varathane Diamond Wood Finish™. It is a water-based acrylic finish (not a varnish or floor wax) for wood, paper, fabric, and other media like our polymer clay. Flecto is the company, Varathane the line, and Diamond Wood Finish the specific kind of product in the line. It actually penetrates the surface of the clay, bonding with it rather than merely coating it. It is water based, easy to apply with a brush, and cleans up with soap and water. It is compatible with the clay and shows no changes or degradation after 10 years of my testing, and it doesn't smell bad—all very important factors. It can also be mixed with pigments, powders and with acrylic paints to form glazes and stains to use on baked clays.

A "stain" typically has far less pigment in suspension than does "paint," and stains are usually applied and then the surface is wiped with a soft cloth to remove the excess. My favorite stains are made with Flecto Varathane as a base and small amounts of black, burnt sienna, and burnt umber acrylic paints, or with Sunset Gold PearlEx™ Powder. These allow me to mimic the finish that accumulates with age on ivory and stone. You can also use blue-greens to mimic verdigris and other metal looks.

Paints mixed in higher concentration can be used to fill in indents in the baked clay, and they look remarkably like enamel when buffed lightly with a piece of polishing cloth. Denim is good for this, as is the T-shirt I use for wiping off stain. After several months of use the fabric is impregnated with the dried stain and is very sturdy in a crinkly way. Eventually it is too crusty to absorb any more stain, but still useful for buffing, so I move on to the next T-shirt as a wiping cloth.

Flecto Varathane can be re-baked if necessary. In fact, the heat seems to fill in tiny brush strokes and "set" the glaze. It can even be used like a glue to hold small pieces in place. I get it in quart cans, fill a clean baby food jar and then work from that. This protects the bulk of the Flecto from contamination or drying. Flecto Varathane seems to dry out faster when mixed with paints or powders, so I generally mix as much stain as I need at a given time, rather than try to keep it fresh for months.

This wonderful product is available in gloss, semi-gloss and satin—which refers to the amount of shine present when it dries. If the lid of the jar you are using becomes cemented in place, run it under hot water for a few minutes and then try again to open it. This usually works to soften any Varathane that is gluing the lid in place. Avoid this occurrence by keeping the jar rim and lid clean and dry. Also, do not wipe your brush against the side of the jar when loading. This action adds air bubbles and gets the jar messy. If you use a soft hair brush to apply surface coatings, you will minimize streaking and bubbles. Use the cheaper plastic bristle brushes when applying stain. Avoid the aerosol. Most spray finishes react badly with clay over time.

When I first starting using polymer clays in 1984, I couldn't find any information about glazes. After my "Great Bead Disaster" (I watched six months of bead making get mushier and stickier as the polyurethane and nail acrylics I had tried as finishes ate the clay) I learned to test for reactions over months and years before committing.

Flecto Varathane has what they call "IPN" or "interpenetrating network" and it goes into the clay itself. To show how important this, I demonstrate the difference in classes that I teach. Several flat, Band-Aid™-sized pieces of clay, (about a #2 thickness on the pasta machine) are baked, cooled, and painted—one with FIMO lacquer, another with Liquitex™ Acrylic Medium (an acrylic paint base), and another with Flecto Varathane™. All are allowed to dry overnight. When the pieces are moved and flexed, the bent FIMO lacquer will flake away, the Liquitex peels off in a "skin" and the Flecto Varathane is fine. Try this and bend them back and forth. You'll see what I mean.

Some artists swear by Future™ Floor Wax, a product available in grocery stores for acrylic floors. I have had no personal experience with it, but many others have had good results that have stood the time test. Any new product that is used with clay should be checked over time to see how it reacts.

Clay can also be sanded and buffed after baking. Use very fine-grade sandpapers and wet/dry sandpapers made for auto finishing. These are best used in a pan or sink full of water, and this also keeps dust from forming. Start with clay that has been stroked with a smooth finger to remove fingerprints prior to baking.

Then, use a fine-grit sandpaper on the baked and cooled clay to further smooth it. Use light, smooth strokes in one direction, not in circles. Use all over the surface and then switch to a higher number grit. This makes the grit finer, almost like gray paper. You should only have to sand with each grit of paper for a few moments before going on to the next. This can be done to remove the top layer of clay and reveal clearer patterns of cane work, or just to give a soft sheen to the clay. Translucent clays can be made almost transparent with sanding and buffing.

When dry sanding use care and a mask to avoid breathing the dust. When using power tools such as buffing wheels, wear protective goggles and a mask. It is very easy to get a bead caught and have it flung at you. While baked clay particles are not poisonous per se, no particulate matter is good for you. Avoid breathing all kinds of dust whenever you can. It is very irritating, and continued inhalation of any kind of dust can cause allergic response, or irritate existing athsma.

I do not personally know of any documented cases of allergic reaction to the clays in contact with skin. Some artists swear by wearing latex gloves while handling the raw clay, but people are statistically more likely to have dermal reactions to the latex and powder in rubber gloves than they are the clay itself. If you prefer to wear gloves anyway, try to get the ones made of nitrile, which do not cause or worsen latex allergies—a fast-growing and extremely serious problem in medical and food workers who must wear them every day. Try to keep your exposure to latex to a minimum. Watch out for the powdered gloves. They are easier to apply, but the powder picks up the latex molecules and makes them breathable. Allergies are more often provoked by inhalation than by skin contact. Always wash after using chemicals or sanding.

tools and supplies

Baking & Safety Tips

Although polymer clays are certified as a non-toxic art material, it is always wise to use common sense and stay on the side of caution. Polymer clays should not be used for items that come in direct contact with food or liquids, including perfume oils or lotions. Nor should they be used on items that will be heated to high temperatures or be in contact with flame. This makes polymer clay unsuitable for dishware or cooking utensils, and a very bad idea for pipes, ashtrays, and even incense holders that may come into contact with burning embers. It is possible to use polymer clays over candleholders or lamps if care is taken to keep them far enough from the heat source. In general, don't cover items meant to get hot or wet.

The most important thing to remember about using polymer clays safely is: *do not overheat!* Each brand has specific times and temperatures that are best. Pieces are baked in a home oven (not a microwave) or large toaster oven at temperatures ranging from 250-275° F. Most small projects require 20 to 40 minutes of baking in a 260° F oven.

There are exceptions to this. The light colors, such as transparent, flesh, porcelain and white (as well as the glow-in-the-darks) are best baked at lower temperatures such as 30 minutes at 250° F. You can re-bake pieces as often as necessary, adding more clay at each stage, and you can reheat items to make them flexible, or softer to cut or carve. Reheat to get beads off of bamboo skewers if they are stuck! (Pull off the reluctant ones while still hot).

Watch out for yellowing or melting. This is not a desirable outcome, and indicates too high a temperature. Although polymer clays must be heated to the proper temperature to harden, scorching can begin at temperatures of 300° F and higher, and at still higher temperatures they release toxic fumes. This is true of all plastics, and is easy to avoid by keeping watch over your oven thermostat. Most are off by a number of degrees, and it is very helpful to purchase an oven thermometer and test the various areas in your oven. Some have corners or spots that are 10° to 75° warmer.

Small toaster ovens are especially variant, and the temperature nearest the heating coil can burn the clay while the other parts of the oven don't get hot enough to cure fully. Also, oven temperatures may go much higher than you'd think when preheating, so check yours before starting anything in a cold oven. I use a large convection toaster oven, and occasionally a home oven for very large pieces. I get best results by being careful.

Slight smoking may occur around 300° F, but this is normal. The toxic fumes are more a problem at 350° F and higher. Burned clay can produce dark, noxious smoke that can irritate and damage your soft tissues, like your eyes and nose or lungs. If you accidentally overheat your oven load and noxious fumes are released, turn off the oven, open the windows and doors, and air out the place. Be careful not to leave a tray of clay in the oven to cool and then have somebody else turn on the oven to start dinner. After such an incident, wipe down the inside of your cooled oven with a soapy washcloth. Then wash the cloth, or dispose of it.

Always work in a well-ventilated area. Use an accurate oven temperature gauge, and your biggest problem should be deciding what to make first.

It's also a very good idea to keep tools you use for clay separate from your normal cooking tools. Although it is possible to use a regular home oven for baking clay, and most people do, always use it at separate times from food preparation. Don't bake the cookies and the beads in the same batch. If you bake frequently, consider getting a separate oven or toaster oven.

Always wash your hands after working with polymer clays, or with any of the powders, inks, finishes and pigments you may use with it. One good way to remove polymer clay residue from your hands is to use baby wipes, or lather your hands with soap and a little water and immediately wipe all of it onto a paper towel or two. Dispose of these, then wash with soap and cold water. Even heavy buildups of clay can be easily removed in this way. It's also a very good idea to regularly use a lotion or conditioner on your hands after washing, as dry skin and rough spots make it harder to smooth your clay projects. You can eliminate the need to sand or at least make it easier to accomplish by having smooth skin and using your finger to "pet" the raw clay into smoothness. Your hands are your most important tools, so take care of them. My personal favorite is Curel™ lotion, but anything that works for you is good.

Surface Stamping

There are many forms of stamps available for use with paper, fabric, and polymer clay. They can be made of carved wood, linoleum blocks, rubber or even metal and stone. Anything that is pressed into the clay to texture it is a kind of stamp. You can make your own or buy them. I collect interesting bits and pieces such as: shells, rocks, textured glass or acrylic from light fixtures or broken tail lights, plastic placemats with lacy patterns, bolts with deep threads, metal moldings, a metal scrubbing pad (clean), some wadded aluminum foil, squares of heavy-grit sandpaper, a baby hair comb, a quilting tracing wheel, and spoons with interesting patterns in the handle or bowl. All these items are used to embellish and mark clay.

Then there are rubber stamps. Foam rubber is used to make some stamps that are particularly nice for walls or fabric, but they are not really suitable for polymer clay. Not only are they not hard enough for good impressions, but the foam rubber reacts with clay fairly quickly. Hard rubber stamps are wonderful to use with paper and with polymer clay. Some acrylic stamps work with both but also react with the clays over time, so you will need to check for deterioration. Hard rubber has been vulcanized—a special heating process that makes it very sturdy.

You can use rubber stamps in so many ways, including pressing them into the clay to make a raised and relief pattern, or by using them to transfer powders and pigments such as PearlEx Powders. These are made by Jaquard Products using mica for the shimmer. FIMO Bronzepulver™ is made by Eberhard Faber using finely ground aluminum. Both products give excellent metallic and pearlescent effects. The colors are more varied with PearlEx. They are wonderful for rubbing onto raised surfaces, or mixing with Flecto Varathane for glazes. The finely ground metal of the

texture sheets

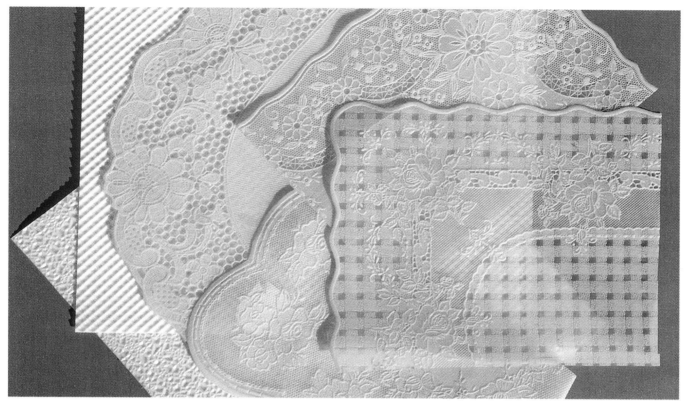

place mats and overhead light fixture plastic

FIMO Bronzepulver requires more care, as you don't want to be breathing it, but it is also is more suitable to fine stamping. The smaller particles of the Bronzepulver allow the stamp to impart a cleaner image.

I put a little of the powder onto a clean, round, plastic lid from a yogurt cup. If you slowly put your rubber stamp into it and press it lightly down a few times, you will pick up a coating of powder without raising clouds of it. After loading the stamp I lightly tap the back of it once with my finger to dislodge any excess or clumps back into the lid. I use care to press cleanly onto the clay area I want to stamp. This should be done as close to baking time as possible. Try not to handle the item much or you can mar the image, or spread the powders. Powders must be protected after baking with a coating of a sealant. I prefer Flecto Varathane, but there are several products that work.

Stamping can also be done using some kinds of stamping inks instead of powders. Inks can be used on raw or baked clay, and can be used just as they are in a decorative way or as guidelines for carving the clay. On baked clay, inks or embossing ink can be used to stamp the image, and then embossing powder can be applied and heated as you would do on paper. You can pop it back in the oven briefly or use a heat gun, but this requires extra caution so as not to singe the clay. Paper burns at 451° F, but polymer clay burns after 350° F.

Many kinds of embossing powders and inks made for use with rubber stamps can be used with clay, but it is always a good idea to test for interaction on a bit of scrap clay. This also gives you a little practice with new materials, so that you can get the feel of it. (Grandma swore by this for making piecrusts, and it's true of any hand-done work. Your brain starts the learning process, but it is when your fingers learn it as well that you can do things with the kind of surety that makes things easier and smoother.)

Rubber stamps can also be used to press the images into a raised relief effect, and powders can be applied to the raised area by dipping a finger into the powder, then lightly rubbing across the surface. Another fabric-like effect can be created by carefully rolling the piece flat again using the pasta roller on a slightly more narrow setting. This gives a brocade look to the piece.

This can also be done using metallic Premo clay with or without added powders on top. Arists such as Mike Buesseler, Pier Voulkos, and Jami Miller have pioneered techniques using the mica displacement effect of Premo, and many others have used these starting points to develop interesting effects. Some look almost holographic.

Other artists, such as Nan Roche, have used stamps and other tools to displace thin layers of clay that are stacked together. The raised areas of clay are then sliced away in a Mokume Gane technique reminiscent of Japanese metalworking. These artists have written about their work in magazines and books, and it is not my intention to duplicate their techniques here, but to encourage you to read more about it.

Clay pieces can also be baked and glazes or stains applied and wiped off for an antique effect, or left pooled to dry and replicate the look of enamels.

You can also press stamps into the clay, then a sharp blade can be used to slice off the top raised bits. Those pieces can be delicately transferred to other pieces of clay, which can be the same or a contrasting color. You can make a carved or filigreed effect in this manner, and though it is a little tricky, this process can be used to build up stunning patterns or embellish other techniques. Stamps or any high-relief item can be used this way. The matrix plates made by Ready Stamps in the process of making rubber stamps are ideal for this, and offer more resistance and bigger area than most stamps.

These delicate-looking filigreed eggs are made with Premo polymer clay baked over real eggshells. The eggs are first blown to remove the contents, washed, and air dried for several days. They are covered with a thin layer of clay at a #5 pasta roller setting (about 1/16 inch) that is wrapped around the shell carefully and fitted to it by removing small triangles of clay around the top and bottom like darts in fabric. I use the leftover ground-up clay from other projects. I use it in many places where it won't be visible. This layer is trimmed of all bumps by paring with a knife or blade. It is then finger smoothed gently, and baked. This makes a very hard egg form that can be covered again with a thin layer of colorful polymer clay.

onlaid eggs

These examples are made with red, green and ivory Premo clay and small amounts of gold foil. The overlay is gold Premo. The mica in the clay gives it a wonderful shimmer. The eggs are covered as before using the colorful layer, and then smoothed with repeated use of fingers and an acrylic rod. They are also carefully rolled between the palms of both hands. The under layer of baked clay allows much more pressure to be exerted, which makes it easier to smooth the layer and not break the shell inside.

It still takes time. However some imperfections can be covered with this onlaid technique, and you can also use gold foils or stamped powders to further decorate this layer and hide minor blemishes. When the surface is smooth enough, run a thin bamboo skewer through the blow holes so the egg can be suspended for decoration and baking.

To make the overlays, press gold clay into rubber stamps or into molds made with clay that have been impressed with rubberstamps and then baked (don't bake your stamps). There will be parts that are raised above the surface of the clay, and those pieces can be sliced free using a tissue blade or Kato's Nu-Blade held parallel to the surface of the clay. Carefully shave the raised portion free and place it on the work surface. Transfer it with a toothpick or knife tip to the surface you wish to embellish. Work one piece at a time and build up a pattern that can be simple or complex. Make sure all edges of the overlay pieces are adhered to the surface of the egg, and not sticking up loose. Use care not to touch the egg much, or you risk squishing the overlays—hold the skewer instead.

When you are satisfied with the design, bake the egg, following package directions. If you wish to close the holes in the egg, you can remove it from the skewer, cover the holes with clay, and bake on a small "nest" of cotton or polyester quilt batting or stuffing such as Fiberfill, which does not burn at low temperatures. To make a musical shaker of the egg, add rice through the top hole before closing and baking. A larger hole and a paper funnel make this job easier.

After baking, antique the egg with a mixture of Flecto Varathane and a small amount of black acrylic paint and metallic gold acrylic paint, or antique gold Pearl-Ex powder. Rub this into portions of the egg as you work, then wipe off the excess with an old clean T-shirt or rag. Allow the egg to dry and use wire or ribbon to make a hanger. You can add tassels or other embellishments as desired.

Unmounted rubber stamps (a sheet of rubber) can be pressed into the raw clay by hand, or rolled through the pasta machine along with a pre-rolled sheet of clay. This can then be cut and applied much like fabric or veneer. It can be stuck to other clay or to forms such as wood, cardboard, papier maché, and to any other items that can withstand 275° F.

You can use commercially made rubber stamps, or take rubber erasers and carve your own with a sharp craft knife. You can also have your own stamps made by one of several companies. My first and favorite choice is Ready Stamps, and every year I have quite a few sets made up especially for me. These feature my own drawings or computer designs, copyright-free clip art, or even the logos of businesses that want promotional items made for them. The stamp, matrix, and plate sets I get from them are some of the best (and most-used) tools in my studio. Since I first discovered Ready Stamps as toolmakers in the early 1990s and wrote about them in the POLYinformER, (the National Polymer Clay Guild's newsletter) many other artists have utilized them in ways I never imagined. I love seeing what people do with these great tools.

The Cerebral Palsy Foundation has a sheltered workshop division in San Diego called Ready Stamps that makes rubber stamps you can order from many office supply stores. You can get uncut and unmounted sheets of rubber stamps made to your original designs, or with copyright-free designs.

If you specifically ask when you order, you can also get the plate and matrix with which it was made. Here's how it works:

• You start with the artwork. You can use original drawings in pen and ink, computer graphic printouts, or computer pictorial elements called dingbats. Some examples used in this book are from a type font called "Fleurons," which is a printer's font that is in the public domain, and therefore free to use. I also often use one called "Kitchen Tile" (created as computer font shareware by Gabrielle Gaither). I manipulated these with a simple graphics program. You can also use photocopies that allow you to play with scale even if you are not using a computer. Reducing designs can make quite a difference.

• You can do your company name, your logo, a signature; or you can use designs from clip art sources and from books such as the Dover Pictorial Archive Series. Dover allows artists to use up to ten designs in a single project without having to seek further permission. Many of the clip art designs found in computers are actually from the Dover Pictorial Archive—you'll begin to recognize them as soon as you've looked at a few of these wonderful books. These designs are seen everywhere in advertising and newsletters.

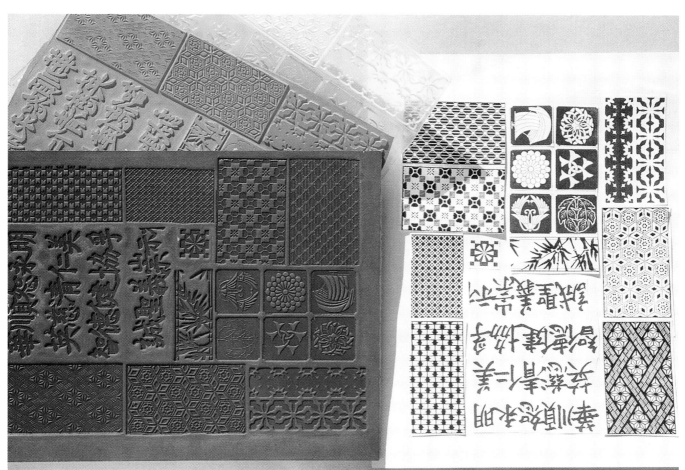

matrix, rubber, and plate plus original art

• Do not try to use copyright-protected material for anything you plan to sell unless you have specific permission. This material includes recognizable cartoon characters originally drawn by someone else. For more detailed and current information about copyright laws you can consult your local library, copyright lawyer, or the Internet.

impressed faux cinnabar tiles and beads

Here are a few tips for best results in ordering Ready Stamps:

• Start with a 9" x 7" rectangle on a sheet of white paper or card stock. Cut out drawn or photocopied images and arrange them inside the rectangle, allowing just a little room between the design elements so that they can be cut apart in the rubber form. Try cutting squares or strips of images with interesting texture patterns. Use images with clear detail and sharp contrast. Avoid hair-thin lines and very large dark areas. When satisfied with your array of designs, paste into place (I use a glue stick). Leave enough room between designs that you can get your scissors between them. The juxtapositions of designs can be very useful in the matrix.

• When mailing, sandwich artwork between two sheets of cardboard so it doesn't wrinkle or smudge. Every mark is reproduced when the stamps are made. Send in your artwork along with $32 (plus $3.00 shipping/handling) for EACH 9" x 7" sheet of artwork.

Remember to specify "plate, matrix, and rubber" when you order. Some people don't use all three, but they are wonderful tools for making texture and pattern in pressed paper or polymer clay. I actually use the matrix far more often than the rubber.

Here's what you get when you order:

Plate: This is a yellow acrylic replica of your 9" x 7" black-and-white artwork, with a raised surface like a stamp, but very hard. It is used to make the next step, the matrix, but is also good to use to press into polymer clay for indented patterns. It can be brittle and cracks easily.

Matrix: This is a brown polymer board, with indented designs. The rubber is poured into this tray and then vulcanized. The matrix is essentially a plate of molds for our polymer clay work. Look at it this way: The matrix is the "inny" version of your designs, and the plate and the rubber are the "outies." You can impress your clay on two sides at once by laying it on the rubber and pressing down on top of the clay with the plate. This is a very useful technique when bead making, or forming other work meant to be viewed in the round.

To use the matrix, it is a good idea to first dust the board very lightly with talcum powder applied with a ponce bag. To make a ponce bag, take a square piece of woven fabric like cotton, place some talcum powder or cornstarch in the center, and bring up all the fabric edges so that the powder is contained in a ball in the center. Close it off with a rubber band, and then use it much like a powder puff to lightly dust molds. This was originally a tool for marking quilting lines through paper templates with colored powders, and is very useful for applying talc as a shallow mold release. Deeper molds, such as those from buttons or doll heads, are better powdered with a plastic bristle brush.

You can press a piece of clay into the matrix and remove the whole piece as a design element. Trim rough edges with a blade or smooth with your finger. Apply to other clay as trim or like decorative molding. You can use pieces as backgrounds, or appliqué elements. Beads can be rolled along the matrix to impress the design, and staining after baking makes for some beautiful faux finish effects.

Mica powders, such as PearlEx™ pigments, can be used to highlight raised areas of impressed clay while the clay is still raw. Acrylic paints available at all hobby and art supply stores thinned with Flecto Varathane™ can be used to fill in baked areas for a faux enamel effect. Water used to dilute paints tends to make bead up, and I have obtained better results with the Flecto™. A little water is OK, but use it sparingly. Or, you can fill in baked areas with soft clay and rebake for an inlaid effect.

Rubber: This is sent to you from Ready Stamps in an uncut sheet, and you can cut and mount it if you so choose. Cut it with scissors around the design elements and then mount with rubber cement or double-sided tape to blocks of wood, foam board, or baked clay handles. You can also cut it into sheets that can be rolled along with the clay through a pasta machine, using the widest setting. Do not bake the rubber. Store your rubber away from sunlight or heat sources. Use a cleaner made for rubber stamps if you use them for inks as well, because soap and water can promote pre-

impressed beads

mature drying and cracking just as it can for your skin.

Commercially made rubber stamps are sold with the idea that people will use them for their own personal use only. It is usually a violation of the copyright law to make items for sale using them. Some rubber stamps are approved for use under what is called an "angel" agreement, but check with the manufacturer first to be sure of a particular stamp's coverage. The standard agreement is that all copies must be hand pulled, meaning no machine use or mass production. Also, the stamps themselves must not be copied. Artists work hard to create the designs made into rubber stamps, and although they want to see them used in beautiful artwork, they still retain the copyrights.

When ordering from Ready Stamps, remember that stamps will reproduce your image as it is seen on the paper, but the matrix is the reverse of it, so if you have words or letters in your design, the image pulled from matrix will be backwards. You can get around this by reversing the original artwork via computer, or by having a transparency made at your printer/copy shop and flipping it over on the copy machine to make an inverted copy. Of course, then you will have a usable matrix and a backwards stamp!

A good example of this is shown in a set that was made during my recent tenure as vice president of Membership for the National Polymer Clay Guild. We wanted to make some promotional pins and other items, so I used a black-and-white copy of the guild logo in three sizes—1", 1 1/4", and 1 1/2". I used a good computer graphics program to play with the sizes. I also made some of them positive (black designs on white background) and some negative (white designs on black background). This is so some have raised letters and some have raised areas around the letters. These were all images that were the right way around on the artwork and recognizable as our logo. Then I reversed some, so that they looked backwards on the artwork. That was so the matrix plate would be a good mold for making pins that had raised and indented portions and could be treated with powders or in other ways.

I cut out the cleanest printouts and used a glue stick to paste them into a 7" x 9" rectangle on a sheet of white paper, and sent it in along with payment. Less than two weeks later, I got my package in the mail. It included my sheet of logo art, a transparency of the art, a red rubber sheet of 27 stamps, a yellow acrylic plate of the designs, and a brown matrix set of molds. All this for less than $40!

I used the matrix and stamps to try out several different techniques and color variations. Our NPCG board members picked out a favorite for this particular project, and our local Colorado guild members went to work to make several hundred pins for promotional use at the next conference. Different techniques and colors can be used to make pins or other applications completely. This is a great way to make promotional items for any group or business.

If we had chosen to have metal pins made by one of many companies that makes promotional items, the cost would have been higher and the results would have been nice but finite. We would have a certain number of pins, and that is all. This way we have had the experience of working together, and we have tools with which to do any number of pins, any time we need them, and to do any number of future projects. This was truly an ongoing and creative solution to our need, and can be adapted to any group's needs.

beads, buttons, and earrings

Carving

Carving baked clay can be made much easier by stamping the design onto the clay first as a guide. Very detailed work can be done this way. Celie Fago and Donna Kato are two artists who have used carving with lovely results.

You can do this using a Dremel™ tool, or by hand with a linoleum cutter or other carving tools. There are many special cutting and carving tools available in art supply stores, and you can even get replacement blades and mount them into a chunk of clay shaped to fit your own grip. This tool should then be baked, and the blade removed carefully and glued back into place.

Some artists decorate their tool handles with clay for easier identification at gatherings and classes, and some do it just because it looks good.

You can carve flat sheets of clay to use as molds or stamps. You can also use this technique much like scraffito, by stacking thin sheets of colored clay and carving down to reveal the hidden layers. Baked, carved clay can be back filled with soft clay, then excess clay is carefully removed with the flat of a blade, making an inlaid kind of effect. Rebake the piece, and sand and buff for a nice luster.

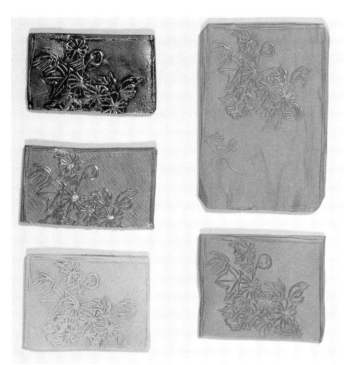

various impressions, carved original

oriental beads, carved & impressed pendants

Other kinds of transfers

Rubber stamps offer an unlimited choice of images to easily transfer to clay, but there's more. You can also use photocopies to decorate clay in amazing ways. Not all copy machines work well, and most laser copier toners do not work well, but the machines they have at the copy center in my town work very nicely. You may have to experiment a little until you find one with the right stuff. Artists like Dottie McMillan and Gwen Gibson have developed transfer techniques using colored copies and even decal-like transfers made with Liquid Sculpey. See their books and videos for more transfer information.

rose transfer, carved box lid, impression

The basics are easy enough and will get you started. You can take any drawing or photograph and make a black-and-white copy, resizing the image if needed. It is best to make the copy slightly dark, but not to the point it is unrecognizable.

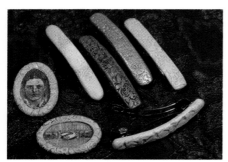

transfer pins, barrettes

At home, cut a piece of the paper containing your image. Don't cut all around the image itself as these lines will impress a faint line into the clay that is not really desirable. Condition and roll a flat piece of clay. Softer clays or those with translucent clay added work best in my experience. Place it on your baking surface so you don't have to move it later. Lay the copied image face down onto the clay and burnish it onto the clay using your finger. Allow it to rest undisturbed for at least 15 minutes. The plasticiser in the clay softens the ink/toner and allows it to transfer to the clay, much as some of us used to do with Silly Putty and the newspaper. Bake the clay with the paper still in place, and then peel off after baking. This gives a stronger transfer than you get if you peel the paper before baking.

Words and other symbols are reversed in the final image and if you want to keep them readable you must first reverse the image before transferring it to the clay. This can easily be done using a computer, or you can have a transparency made at a copy shop. Use the transparency to make copies on paper, first reversing the transparency so that the copy seems backwards. It'll be right-way-around in the final image.

Transfers can be used to make special family heirlooms. How about holiday ornaments using your child's school picture? Or a treasure box with a copy of the wedding photo of your parents or grandparents worked into the lid? One caution—photos are also reversed in the transfer process, and this can throw off the recognition function in our brains, especially with familiar images. Grandma doesn't look quite the same in reverse, and so it may be a good idea to have a transparency made first, then the image on the clay will match the remembered one from the photo.

Transfers can be left as they are, or colored in using pencils or felt-tip pens. Some brands will bleed into the clay over time, so do test your markers and other materials on a piece of baked clay that is allowed to age for a bit to establish compatability if there is any doubt. Berol Prismacolors work well.

colored rose transfer tray

You can also color the paper with these before transferring to the clay, but the effect is more subdued. Oil pastels also can be used to draw designs on paper, which can then be transferred to the clay. You can make baked pieces of clay with transfers and store them for later use, re-baking them into bigger pieces or gluing into place. This is a good technique to use in making decorative pieces to add to photo albums or personal journals.

Making Molds

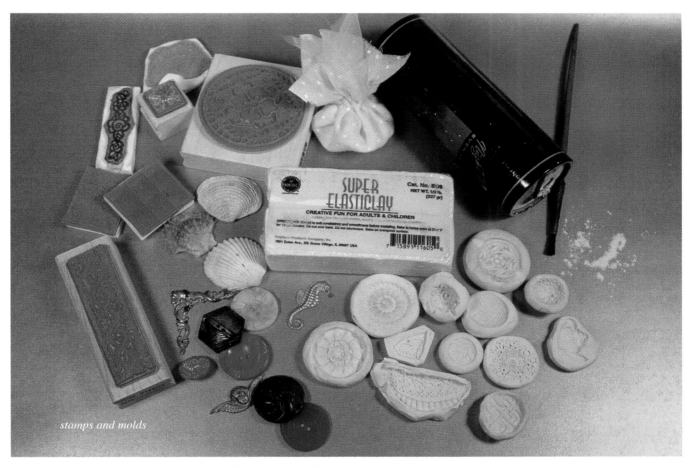

stamps and molds

Polymer clay can be hand modeled or used with molds. It can also be used to make very good molds. There is a particular kind of polymer clay called Super Elasticlay, made by Polyform Products, which also make Sculpey, Premo, and SuperFlex Clays, that works well for molds. While all polymer clays can be used to make molds, Super Elasticlay and SuperFlex retain pliability after baking. The mold is not rigid, and this allows you to "pop" the piece out of the mold more easily. It also makes it possible to mold areas with undercuts such as doll noses and chins, and still obtain good pressings from the molds.

My own preference is Super Elasticlay, and I have made hundreds of molds with wonderful results. In fact, at one time I carried some in my purse wherever I went, just in case I found a texture I had to have. I have been known to go to dinner with friends, and take impressions of their flatware or doorknobs. To facilitate this, I also carried powder and a soft cloth—it

seemed a natural progression after years of carrying a diaper bag!

Super Elasticlay is much softer than other clays, and is still pliable when baked. There are several things to remember when using it or other clays as a mold. The first is to always follow the manufacturer's baking directions. Elasticlay is sensitive to over baking. Also, cool the piece completely before touching or moving it from the baking pan, as it is not completely stable until cooled.

To make a mold, first use talcum powder or cornstarch and a paintbrush to completely powder your original. This is vital, as the Elasticlay is sticky and will adhere to any unpowdered surface. It can be removed with a toothbrush and a soft cloth if you forget this—but it takes an effort. Use a lump of Elasticlay that has been kneaded a few times—although it does not require as much conditioning as other polymer clays, it still takes some. Use a piece larger than your original, so that you have enough for "walls" around the outside, and so that the original does not push through the bottom. Press the powdered original into a slightly flattened ball of Elasticlay (or other clay if you so choose), firming the sides of the molding clay around the original, but not engulfing it, and then pull the original straight up and out of the mold.

If you have not gotten a good cast of the original, ball the mold clay up, re-powder the original, and try again. When you have a good casting, you can trim away excess mold clay if desired, and then bake the mold according to directions. It is possible to bake some originals along with the mold, but I usually do not, as I want to check for any air bubbles or other problems first. I find that Elasticlay takes a finer impression than other polymer clays, and has far fewer air bubbles or other defects than plaster of Paris, a common molding compound.

Whatever you use to make your molds, using them well often requires a mold release. Again, I prefer talcum powder, which I use with a ponce bag or paint brush to very lightly coat the mold. Then, use a conditioned ball of clay to press into the mold. I like to find the right amount of clay for each mold so that there is not a lot of excess to be trimmed away, and the piece is flush with the top of the mold. To remove it from the mold, I use another "pusher" piece of clay, a larger lump that is pressed onto the exposed back of raw clay. This sticks to it a bit, and the piece comes out of the mold easily. It can then be gently eased or sliced from the pusher and placed in a pan for baking.

Two molds can be used together to form pressed

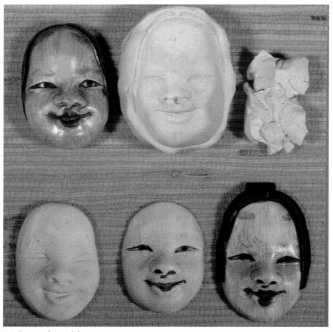

Noh mask mold steps

faces from the Noh mold

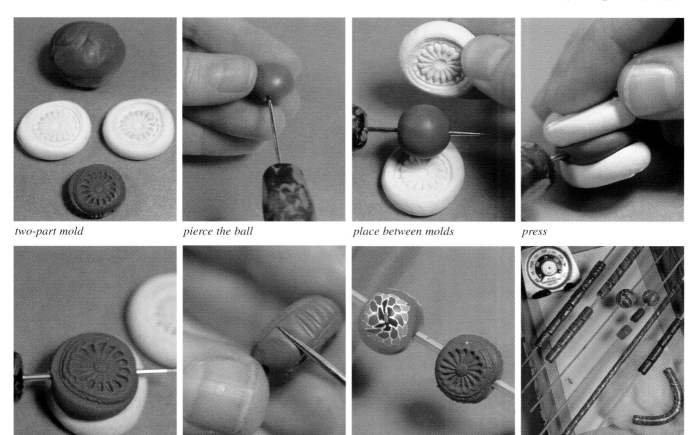

two-part mold *pierce the ball* *place between molds* *press*

remove from mold *score sides* *thread onto skewer* *ready for baking*

items. I often make beads this way by taking a round ball of clay skewered on a toothpick or bead reamer, placing it into one mold with the skewer running across the top, and gently pressing the other mold down onto the clay. By trapping the skewer in between the two molds it serves to keep the hole in place. This helps you make sure the molded design is not deformed while you try to skewer the bead—it's much easier to skewer first. When removed from the molds, the seam between the two molds can be smoothed or impressed further with a knife blade, rubber stamps or other texture tools.

Rubber stamps can be used to make flat sheet molds, much like the matrix trays from which the stamps themselves were made. Start with a thick, flat piece of scrap clay if you have it, or any color you are willing to use. I like to use a #1 thickness, or two stacked together for deeper impressions. Trim the edges to make a rectangle of even depth. Use rubber stamps or any texture item—nail heads, screens, metal trims or old jewelry—to press down into the clay. Powder the item lightly, then press straight down and pull up again smoothly. This helps to make a mold of even depth and angle.

You can use single images or string several together to make a border or frame. You can place several

images in proximity and then use a knife or other carving tool to connect the images with lines, dots, curls or other hand cut patterns. This can be done before or after baking. Doing it after yields a crisper line when carving and helps keep the stamped images from being marred while you're working other portions of the design.

The finished flat molds can be used to make raised images of the original stamp. These can be used as is, or can be sliced free of the clay plug used to make them and applied to other clay. These are very useful molds. A great deal of time and clay can be used making them, but they are a lot of fun to create and to use.

You can do the same thing onto a thinner sheet of clay (such as a #4 setting) and texture it with lace or cloth or even raised patterns on paper, and use the baked texture sheet to roll through the pasta machine along with a pre-rolled sheet of clay. Begin by rolling the clay to a #2, then put the clay and the texture sheet through the machine together on a #1 setting. If you don't use a pasta machine, you can still use these pieces by placing them on top of the clay and using a roller to impress the design. Experiment to find the way they work best for you. Some work better when you press the clay onto the texture. Some are best done by pressing the texture onto the clay.

Pieces can be stamped or molded and baked, and then inserted into larger pieces of raw clay to make more complex designs. They can also be used to make jewelry and collage components.

texture beads

Part II
Canes

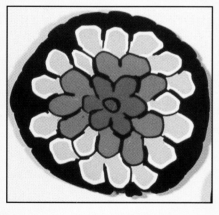

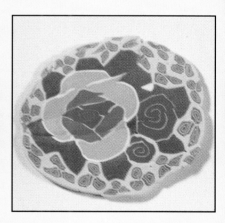

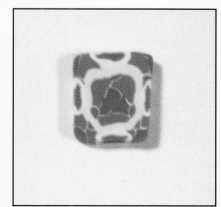

Geometric and Floral Cane Work

Cane work is actually a Venetian glass-making term. It refers to the use of long rods of colored glass that are melted together and then sliced as-is for some kinds of Italian art glass, or drawn out while still hot to reduce the pattern in scale, and sliced. These slices are then often applied to more molten glass, forming beautiful marbles, paperweights, jewelry and other glass artifacts.

This ancient process is often used to make floral patterns, and came to be referred to as "millefiore" (literally "thousand flowers" in Italian). It is still done by expert glassmakers today and artisans have expanded far beyond the simple daisy with which many begin.

This process of building up a pattern with differently colored parts and then slicing off pieces to use decoratively is also used in Yosegi, a Japanese woodworking technique. Intricate geometric patterns are built up out of strips of different woods bundled carefully together, then sliced across the top and used in ultra-thin sheets as veneer for intricate boxes, decorative items and furniture.

Caning is also used in some kinds of pastry and candy making, especially hard sugar candies. Cinnamon rolls are a kind of cane work—flat white rectangles of dough are layered with a brown topping of sugar and spice, then rolled up and drawn out by means of light steady pressure on the tube of what will become rolls. These are sliced and baked, with each one showing the same distinctive spiral pattern. This can also be done with clay, and the jelly roll or spiral is one of the first canes many people make.

Italian glass brooch

Polymer clay artists have borrowed from the best, and made millefiore part of our artistic toolbox. I have an antique Italian brooch that was brought home from a European visit by my grandmother. It was this brooch that first alerted me to the possibilities of putting clay patterns together like tiny puzzle pieces.

An article in *Ornament Magazine* many years ago by Tory Hughes explained in detail about the millefiore technique and how it could be used with polymer clays, and I realized that the decorative possibilities were huge. It opened up new vistas and creative realms far beyond the doll making and miniature sculpture that I was already exploring. In fact, miniature makers have use polymer clay in this way for many years, using canes to make tiny orange slices, candies, etc. These tiny canes are often baked before slicing, as the blade easily goes through and the hardened cane does not deform at all when slicing each small piece.

Canes made of polymer clay are put together like puzzles with different-colored pieces. They are reduced by diligently working the clay to extrude it, making it longer and thinner without distorting the pattern. This is done with glass by heating the rods and pulling them outward. With clay, the process requires tricky handling so as to move the clays outward without moving them around so much that the pattern is lost or deformed beyond recognition.

The larger the component pieces are at the beginning, the more detail can be built in, and the more difficult it is to reduce effectively. Some artists build canes of breathtaking complexity, and some use simple canes so effectively that the finished work is far more beautiful than the original cane would lead you to expect.

Imagine a child's wooden puzzle of the United States. Ohio is a blue, wooden piece, right next to a red West Virginia piece, snuggled up against a green Kentucky piece, and so on. These individually shaped pieces fit next to each other to form the bigger pattern that is the United States. If those same pieces were formed of clay, and perhaps 3 inches deep instead of the 1/2 inch deep or so of the wooden pieces, then it would be the beginnings of a cane. If that cane were squeezed and pulled and worked until it was much longer (deeper) and much smaller in diameter than it began, this would be a "reduced cane" and the pattern of the United States would still be there in each slice, although much smaller than the original design. Of course, this requires great care in the building and reduction process, or you could end up with the tip of Florida wrapping around the Great Lakes.

Such large shifts in the pattern can be acceptable in some canes, particularly florals. It is not so in face canes, where you want the mouth to stay under the nose and not migrate to somewhere up by the forehead. It is best to start with simple floral and geometric canes, and practice building and reduction techniques before moving on to more ambitious projects such as faces or words.

Bull's-eyes are also easy to make this way. Simply roll a snake of one color and wrap it in an even sheet of another color. Marie Segal showed me a neat trick for knowing where to cut this sheet to make it butt evenly, rather than overlapping and making one part thicker. Take the snake, place it on a rectangular sheet, and begin to roll. Keep going until the edge you started with hits the clay sheet again. The cut edge will make a faint mark on the raw clay of the sheet that you will see if you unroll it just a little. Use your knife to cut along this line, and wrap the snake neatly! Use your finger or thumb to smooth the seam a little, and continue to roll a bit to fuse it all together, making sure you didn't trap any bubbles. You can stop there, or continue wrapping in layers to make concentric circles. A snake of black, wrapped in a layer of white, and then another layer of black, then sliced and placed on a ball of black clay will appear to be a white ring floating in space. This same slice placed on a white lump of clay will appear to be black polka dot on white, floating inside a black ring.

Stripes can be made by stacking flat sheets of different-colored clay. You can go far beyond this simple effect by cutting and recombining pieces. For instance, a checkerboard can be made by stacking sheets of white, black, white, and black. Trim the edges of this striped cane to make it an even rectangle. Cut this into even slices down the length of the cane—like bacon—and each section will be a rectangle of white, black, white, black stripes. Lay one face down on the work surface, and pick up the next. Flip it so that it is now black, white, black, white, and carefully place it so that the black bit is over the white bit of the first piece. Continue like this and you have a checkerboard pattern which shows in each slice from the end of the cane.

Another fun thing to do with stripes is to roll up the stack like a jelly roll, or around a snake like the bull's-eye. Take a few long slices of it, as in the checkerboard, and place this around a snake. It gives the effect of radiating lines outward from a circle. This is good for flower centers or sunbursts.

You can also easily make very thin stripes by stacking up two or more colors in sheets, then running this through the pasta roller on the widest setting. This makes the sheet longer and compacted in depth. Cut rectangles from this sheet and stack to form pinstripes. This is also a very good way to make faux bone (use layers of ivory, white/translucent) or faux wood (use browns and very thin layers of black). For these faux effects it is a good idea to use some layers of clay that are not precise. I roll them by hand, leaving some areas thicker for a natural variance to the "grain."

These simple geometric patterns can be used to build up far more complex images, and lengths of canes can be sliced lengthwise down the middle to form half circles from circles, or triangles from squares. These can then be further manipulated to build a dizzying array of complex patterns. You can keep an interesting record of your canes by cutting a few slices of each as you make them, and baking. Keep them all in a bowl or jar, or try pressing a raw slice or two of each onto a sheet of solid-color backing or scrap clay, then rolling the resulting collage flat. Trim and bake as flat "pages." These can even be scanned before or after baking and used as images for other artistic purposes, such as making your own gift wrappings, cards or T-shirts using a computers and printer.

Always start cane building with more clay than you think you will need, especially if you are using a custom mix color. It is better to have leftovers than to try to remember what the formula was for that special shade.

Although I began by building very tiny canes that only yielded a dozen or two slices, I quickly came to understand the process required more size for more detail, and recombining eats up large amounts of simple canes. I went from making canes that started at the size of a pill bottle and yielded perhaps 12 inches of cane to making my standard canes about the size of a soft drink can. These yield perhaps 3 feet of finished cane or more. Some of my canes, especially ones I do not wish to have to repeat making very often and need in quantity, I make using as much as 10 pounds of clay at a time.

This is particularly true for my face canes. They begin around the size of a three-layer cake. My last Japanese girl face cane took 12 pounds of raw clays, and six hours of work to build. It took another eight hours to reduce, and this took both my husband and myself at the beginning, working with four hands together to carefully squeeze the clay towards its own center, without pushing too hard.

I was very lucky to end up with almost 10 pounds of usable cane, and the 2 pounds that were on the ends of the cane, and too distorted, were all reclaimable as individual colors salvaged out, or as "schmutz." This byproduct of caning is unavoidable, though it can be minimized by careful building and reduction. This is a chance to practice "positive point of view." Don't look

at it as wasted clay, because it is most useful in many ways. It can contain a secondary cane image that you did not actually plan but find interesting, or it can be used to make companion striped/marbled parts for your cane. (Natasha style beads, named after their original creator, use this kind of clay to great effect!) It can be reclaimed into component colors if the parts are big enough. It can be processed together to form a new color. Or, if you find the color is unacceptable in your

palette, use it to form cores for larger pieces, as backing for appliquéd slices for pins or covering other items such as box lids. It's very valuable stuff! In fact, we never seem to have enough.

The most important step of cane building is to pack all clay components firmly together so they do not shift during reduction. Start with clays of the same consistency so they reduce evenly. It is also vitally important to start large enough. Canes with a starting depth of less than 2 inches are difficult to manipulate, and don't result in many good slices. A good cutting tool like the JASI Slicer (designed by Judith Skinner of The Skinner Blend fame) is invaluable for making extremely even slices and for getting the last few slices out of a cane. We use this tool all the time, especially when making buttons, which need to be the evenly sliced throughout the set.

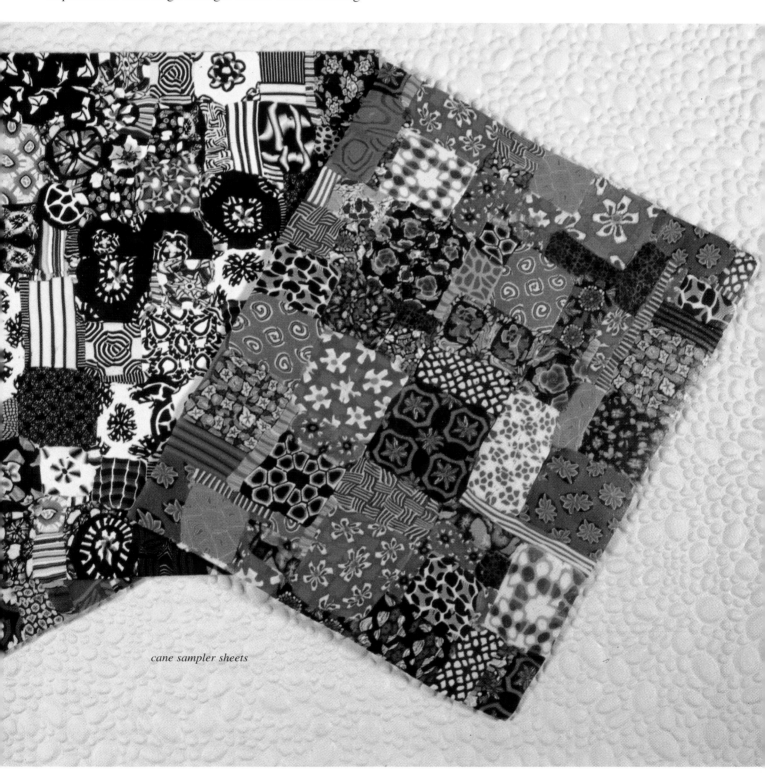

cane sampler sheets

Floral Canes

Books or periodicals about flowers are a great place to look for inspiration. You can also find floral patterns everywhere around you—in fabric designs, on the tissue box, in advertisements for decorative items.

Then there are seed catalogs, books on wallpaper designs or vintage textiles and, of course, your imagination.

Most flowers have a center, some kind of petals, and leaves. These parts can be combined to depict real existing flowers, or to come up with your own fantasy flora. Changing the colors of each part or using different background colors makes each cane unique. No matter what design you choose to make, the fundamentals of shaping the components, packing them, and reducing them are the same.

chrysanthemum maiden necklace

pink chrysanthemum (pt. 1)

Stamens can be made by taking a narrow triangle-shaped snake of your petal color. These are made of snakes that have been turned into triangle shapes by pinching the top together as you flatten the bottom by pushing it down on the work surface. Then run a strip of stamen color—white, black, yellow or gold are some good choices—down the length of two sides of the triangle, meeting at the point if desired, but not covering one side of the triangle, which becomes the outside. Place a thin strip of petal color over stamen layer. You should now see a "V" of stamen color, with petal color surrounding. Do this to an entire snake before cutting it into the lengths desired. Cut this into equal lengths, and place together with points in the center, so that the "V's" radiate out like wheel spokes. You can use a snake in the center here as well, with V's radiating out from it.

Cherry blossoms and wild roses are two flowers with a circular ring of stamens. Reduce a bit to the desired size before using to build the rest of the flower. You may well have too much for one flower, but you can use leftovers later in a different one.

Petals—Some flowers, such as poppies, have only three or five petals. Chrysanthemums can have hundreds. Other flowers fall somewhere in between. The simplest way to make a petal is to make a long round snake, then point one end into a teardrop. You can pinch a lot, all the way down the snake, to make thin petals, or leave them wider for fewer petals. It is best to use a blunt point for a large-centered flower, and thinner points for a small-centered flower.

Cut the snake into equal portions and fit around the center, radiating outward. Make small triangle snakes of background color. Fit them into the divots between petals to keep them in place, otherwise the petals will meld together into a solid shape and lose their distinctions. Petals can also be wrapped in a darker or lighter color for more visibility. I often wrap light-colored components in black sheets of about a #5 thickness, or use white for wrapping darker components. When reduced, these are like drawn pen outlines.

Wrap the entire petal snake before cutting to save time and effort. You can add stripes (veins) of color to the petals when building the petal snake in the same way as making stamens. Just use petal colors and layer as many pieces onto the wedge sides, but not the top, as you like. White and purple are very nice this way, as are other combinations. This makes vertically shaded or striped petals

To make horizontally shaded petals, such as magnolias, start with the darkest or lightest of three or more petal colors. Roll out a snake, then wrap in the next colors, going to lighter or darker as you choose. These

Centers—Some centers are a simple circle in the middle of a flower, such as is seen in daisies. This is made with a single snake of your choice of color. It is best to have a lot of contrast in the colors as reduction makes things smaller and less obvious. I often use black, white, or gold for centers. Another form is a bull's-eye, with a wrapped snake forming the piece. These can also be reduced a bit and put together to form multiple little spots in the final center.

Roses have a spiral or jelly roll center, which is particularly effective when you start with a wedge of the flower color rather than a flat piece. Next comes a thin sheet of much darker or lighter clay placed on top. Roll it up starting with the thin portion of the wedge, so that the thick part is on the outside. You can do it with the wrap on the outside, or tucked into the spiral, whichever you prefer. This makes a simple little rose all by itself, which is lovely next to full-blown roses with petals, or in bouquets with other flowers.

layers don't have to be the same width. In fact, it is nicer if they are not. If you start with the darkest of the shades, you would next wrap in the medium, then with next lightest, and so on. If you start with the lightest, you would gradate towards the dark on the outside. Both are lovely, just be sure to maintain your direction of light to dark.

When you have built your snake as desired, finish with a #5 wrap of contrasting color such as white or black. Cut down the length of the snake to form two half circle snakes. You can use them just like this for petals, or cut down the length again for quarter circles. For petals, you can shape them a bit more like teardrops and less like wedges, or use them as is for rose petals, which are layered around a spiral center.

Another option is to not shade the petals them-selves, but use light, medium, and dark snakes to make petals, and layer them outward from the center. The rose cane and the chrysanthemum cane are examples of this. The amount of reduction done to these canes makes individual gradations within the petal difficult to see, but the three or four layers of petals perform the same shading function in the finished flower.

Leaves—These can be as simple as green wedges, or as complex as ferns. They start as green snakes, and can have central veins, horizontal veins, outline wraps—whatever you choose! The more detailed leaves are made of simple components that are reduced and cut, then placed together in a pattern. I like to arrange these complex leaf components radiating out-ward from a "stem," which is a strip of green standing on edge. Leaves look very natural when you use them in place of a few of the background wedges in between the flower petals.

Background—Background clay is used to fill in all the spaces between the components. That's one reason you need so much of it. It can be solid color or simple canes that combine to form a patterned backdrop. The background clay is what keeps the shapes you have formed in place. The complex rose cane shown in this book uses a cream and gold jelly roll cane for the background fill. The chrysanthemum cane has a solid fuchsia background.

pink chrysanthemum (pt. 2)

Reduction

The most important part of successful reduction is correct building before reduction! It is absolutely vital that all the clays in a cane be of similar consistency. If one color is hard, and one is soft, they will reduce unevenly, with the soft color moving very quickly, and the hard moving little or not at all.

Also, packing background clay around the various bits and pieces must be done so that there are no holes showing. The clay will move around to fill any spaces, and not in ways that you plan. The clay on the outside of your cane gets the most pressure applied, so you must protect your design elements. I usually wrap a final outer layer of clay around my canes so that there is at least a 1/4-inch layer between design parts, like flower petals, and the edge.

This is particularly important for face canes. Otherwise, the central parts, like the nose, reduce very little compared to the outer parts and you get little squinty eyes and lips, and a huge honker! With face canes, I usually wrap as much as a whole pound of black or flesh around the face cane before reducing. Much of this layer gets pulled out to the very ends of the cane by the time reduction is done, and what started out as a 1/2-inch layer of black looks like a fine black outline by the time I'm done. Most of the ends of the reduced cane are solid black, and instead of being most of the eyes and mouth, the black can be salvaged back into use easily, and my cane looks more as I intended it to look.

Another very important thing to do before reduction is to rest the cane. The bigger the cane, the longer it needs to rest. I always try to impress this on my students, and I have learned the hard way not to ignore my own advice. I would go home, curious as could be, and think "Well I'm the teacher, I'll just reduce this now because I want to see how it turned out." Then it would not reduce well at all, reducing me to tears on occasion. Now I know better.

If your cane is bigger around than your wrist, let it sit for at least an hour or two, and if it is bigger than 6 inches in diameter, let it sit overnight. This allows the outside of the cane to become the same temperature as the inside. You've been working the outside the most recently, so it is warmer and more pliable, plus the outer layer gets the most pressure, so it moves much faster and easier than the inside. This is particularly important for faces, although a flower moved around a bit is OK. You can manipulate the image to deliberately distort it. You can also cut and add or change some proportions and things in a kind of "plastic surgery."

I start the reduction of large canes while they are still standing upright, like a soft drink can. I use both hands on opposite sides of the cylinder to press towards the middle, condensing it inwards and moving my hands and the cane as I go. I do this until it is at least taller than my hands. Sometimes, especially with whopper-sized canes, I use my roller (a piece of acrylic pipe) like a rolling pin. A piece of PVC pipe will do. I put the bottom of the pipe on my work surface, perpendicular, standing upright, like the cane, and use my hand to roll it around the circle, pressing again towards the center of it all. I use my other hand to hold the cane in place, for resistance. I do this to smooth out the ridges before they become pronounced. You want to keep things moving smoothly.

When my cane pillar has become tall enough, I flop it over, laying it on my clean work surface, otherwise all those little bits you didn't notice before get embedded, so that it is a "snake" in front of me. If it is more than 2 or 3 inches thick, I pick it up, and smack it down onto the table, then roll it a quarter turn so a different part of the surface hits the table. Do this several times. This jolts the clay all the way through to the center of the cane. This is a very useful technique to try when your clay is stiff and refuses to reduce.

The Roll-y Part

To continue, I lay my fingers on the cane, with both hands starting in the center, and roll it back and forth, moving my hands slowly apart and outward towards the ends as I go. Then I give the whole cane a quarter turn so I work a different surface. No part should get too much attention at one time. If you can see deep finger ridges, you are pressing too hard. You have to

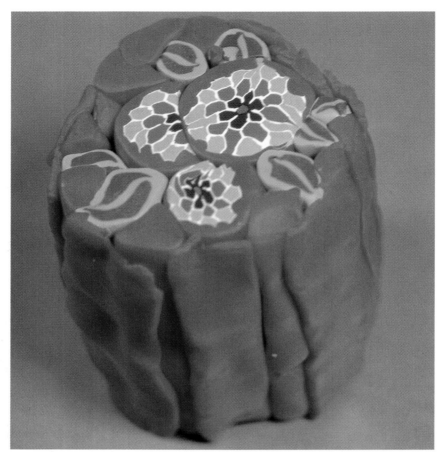

*complex purple
chrysanthemum cane*

gently press down as you roll, moving towards the ends, but not too much. Then flip the cane, end to end, so that what was the right end is now the left end. Do this so that you counteract the "drift" of the clay, which can result in lopsided faces, etc. Now do the roll-y thing some more.

Remember to keep moving and flipping the cane once in a while. It takes time and patience. Remember, the faster it goes, the more distortion occurs. If at any time you feel the clay "slipping" or moving funny inside the cane, you may have an air pocket. When this occurs, squeeze the cane gently down on itself, against your work surface, pressing the outside towards the center gently. Obvious bubbles can be popped with a pin, and the air pocket carefully pressed out.

The Squeeze-y Part

I alternate the rolling technique with a squeeze technique, especially with big canes or canes that are not moving along. Hold the cane in mid air with both hands. Let one end dangle. Using both hands, placed like you are climbing a rope, work your way down the cane squeezing and compressing the cane in on itself. As I work down the length of it, I let the top part of really big canes rest over my shoulder.

Flip it end to end, and repeat. You can also work

your way up. This technique can look very odd, but it works. Remember this about reduction: not too hard, and not too fast. Gravity helps, but can work against you if the cane gets too soft. Let it rest and cool a few minutes, if need be.

I almost always alternate between the roll-y thing and the squeeze-y thing. Rolling helps keep you from getting divots from your fingers, squeezing helps get things to move. You must be careful not to squeeze too much in one place. If your cane is getting too long (more that a couple of feet) cut it in half, and work each piece separately. Resist the temptation to cut off your ends, though. Ends are always distorted, but they protect the rest of the cane. What becomes an end becomes distorted. You can run out of cane this way, so leave those ends on when you can until you have reduced close to your desired diameter.

Once a cane is less than 2 inches in diameter, I usually concentrate more on rolling, rather than squeezing. I have reduced canes down to 1/4 inch in diameter with these techniques; it just takes practice, and patience. Giant sized canes require 4 hands to reduce—my husband and I work together to manipulate them. It takes time and effort, but then we have lots of slices with which to work, and each cane is its own adventure.

compress

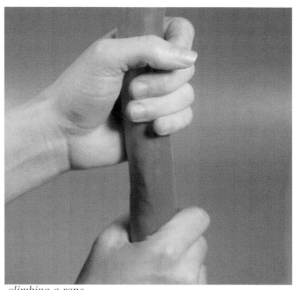

climbing a rope

roll

ends

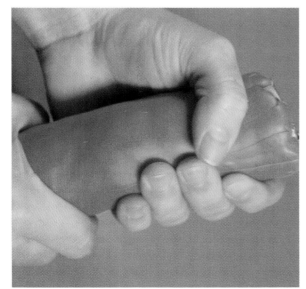

squeeze

secondary cane

The Chrysanthemum Cane

premo chrysanthemum cane

Simple and Complex Canes

Only by making a large amount of cane will you be able to manipulate it in various ways to form more complex patterns. By combining and re-combining, endless designs are possible.

The Chrysanthemum Cane

This cane is shown in two color ways—pinks with black background, and purples with fuchsia background—so that you can see how altered the same design appears when done in different colors.

I did the chrysanthemum petal colors in three layers: Dark at the center, then a row of medium, then light, with a highlight layer of white on the edge of the petals. You need very little of the center color (I chose gold) and two 2-ounce blocks or more of the dark color and 2 ounces each or more of light and dark green, as well as a much larger amount of white for mixing petal colors and outlines. I picked fuchsia for mixing and for the background. Since the cane size you choose may vary, this will not be a mathematically precise recipe—so don't get out the scale. You just need more of the outer layer color, and less of the inner layers. And most of all you need background!

For the dark petals I used half my purple formed into a long snake as fat as my index finger. To the remaining purple, I added some fuchsia and white and rolled it into a snake at least twice as long as the dark snake. This is my medium petal snake. I cut the final inch or so from each end of this medium color snake, and mixed it with enough white to make a much lighter tint, of which you need at least twice as much as the medium. Your dark, medium, and light tones should be easily distinguishable from each other—if not, darken or lighten as needed by adding more white or original color.

Form the light color into a snake as well. Using the pasta machine at a thin setting—#5, on my machine—I cranked out a "tongue," or strip, of white, and layered this on top of the light snake. Don't layer all the way around. You want a strip of the petal color showing at the bottom of the snake. Smooth the parts together, making sure no air is trapped to form bubbles. Pop the ones that exist and smooth together.

The next step is to reduce this snake somewhat until it is only slightly bigger in diameter than the dark and medium snakes. It may seem as though there is an awful lot of clay there, but you'll need it.

Cover the dark and medium petal snakes with the thin layer of white as well, again leaving the very bottom of the snake uncovered. Don't worry about slight imprecision or raggedy bits at this point. It'll never show when the cane is finished.

To make the chrysanthemum cane you will need: clay for the center, petals, leaves, and background.
Condition the clays and mix all colors completely.

For this project, I started with the following colors:
- 2 oz. purple
- 2 oz. light green, about the same of dark green and a tiny amount of gold
- 1 lb. white (only about half was used)
- 1 lb. fuchsia (all but a few ounces was used)

I ended up with the following amounts of cane:
single flower:
    1/2" diameter—13" length
    3/4" diameter—4" length

complex flower with leaves:
    1" diameter—6 1/2" length
    5/8" diameter—16" length

complex leaf (from leftovers):
    5/8" diameter—8" length

single square:
    3/4" diameter—6" length

complex square:
    1" diameter—3 1/4" length

There were also about 2 to 4 ounces from the ends of canes

Forming the Flower Cane

Roll out the center color (I chose gold) into a snake. Put it aside, then lightly pinch the bottoms of the dark, medium and light snakes so that they are more teardrop shaped than round, with the point of the teardrop showing the petal color. Cut your dark snake into six equal lengths, about 2-3 inches, then use one piece to measure the same length pieces on the medium color. Get as many pieces of equal length as you can, reducing the snake a little if need be on some, to make them long enough. I used nine pieces.

Cut the light snake into two sections. Set one portion aside, and reduce the other, stretching it out a bit to make roughly the same size petals as the medium and dark. Cut to the same length pieces. Cut the center (gold) snake to the same length as well. I try to start with at least 2- or 3-inch-long pieces when building a cane so I have enough. Sometimes they are much longer.

Place petal snakes around the center piece so that they have the point side touching the center, rounded end out, and run evenly down the length of the center snake, enclosing it neatly. This should use up your dark snake. Then place the medium petal pieces evenly around the outside of the first layer. Place the points of

purple mum cane colors

just slice like cheese

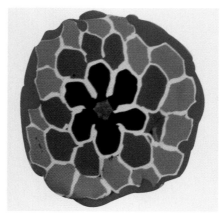

purple mum

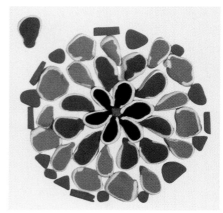

in sections

center

dark, medium, light

reduced

with fuchsia

reduced

reduced and flattened

complex cane sections

reduced

reduced further

pinched snake

cut in half, wrapped

leaf cane

pinch end to point

make two halves

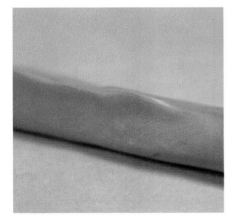

triangle snake (background)

cut to length

fill in the background

the pieces in the "V" divots of the preceding layer and skip one or two grooves as needed to go around the entire circumference evenly. Fill these in with light pieces in the same way. The remaining pieces will be used in the outer layer.

Take the larger light snake that remains and use your forefingers and thumbs to flatten the point while widening the snake so that the outermost petals will be wider and a little more squat. The next layer will be built in the same way as the others, using the remaining light pieces around the circumference. You can, if you choose, add more layers and more gradations, but this does take more clay.

Fill in all remaining grooves with triangle snakes of background color (I used fuchsia). Make triangle snakes by pinching the top of a small round snake while pushing it down onto your work surface. Take the entire cane into your hands and gently squeeze up and down the length of it, inwards and onto itself, to urge the clay together and move out any air. Check the top and bottom faces of the cane to make sure they are properly aligned all the way through the cane and that everything is placed where you want it.

Roll out a #1 thickness sheet of background color clay, and wrap the entire length of the cane. Do it twice, if you have enough clay. This protects the image, as the outermost layer of clay shifts and changes the most during reduction. Don't skimp on the wrapping. You get less distortion and more usable cane if you use a protective wrap, much of which will wind up at the ends of the cane after reduction.

Roll the entire cane gently to smooth the form, and make sure the wrap is attached well with no air pockets. Then let the cane "rest" for an hour before you reduce it. This allows the outside layer to cool off a bit so that the inside and outside will be reduced more evenly, and it lets the various parts of the cane adhere to each other somewhat.

Reduce the cane, and after reduction cut off the first inch or two on either end. Keep slicing until you come to a clear image. This is the simple chrysanthemum cane! Keep these cut-off bits. They are useful.

To Make The Leaf Cane

Roll either your light or dark green into a thumb-sized diameter snake. It's your choice—one will be the leaf, the other will be the vein and wrap. A dark wrap is good against a light background, and a light one works well against a dark background. Pinch the ends a bit for a leaf shape.

Cut down the length of the leaf snake, to make two half-circle snakes. Use the pasta roller (set at #4) and roll out a long tongue of the other green. Cut an inch-wide strip as long as the leaf snake and apply it sandwich style between the two cut leaf pieces. Trim away any excess. Roll out the left-over vein into a tongue again and wrap the leaf cane entirely. Reduce this to the diameter of the flower or less, then pinch the top and bottom where the vein is to form the round cane into a more leaf-like shape again.

Next, cut as many sections as you can to 3 or 4 inches. Reduce a few sections if needed to get the full length. Different-sized leaves are the result, and they will look more natural. Take a leaf piece and cut down the length of it at right angles to the vein. It's easiest if you stand the section up on end so that you look down on the face of it as you slice down. Little variances make it more natural here as well, so don't worry if you are not totally precise.

To Make The Complex Cane

Cut the flower cane into sections. You want two pieces about 1 inch in diameter, and 3 inches in length. Wrap what is left in plastic wrap to keep them from drying out and put them aside for later.

Reduce one of the flower pieces to a diameter of 3/4 inch or so, and trim it to the 3-inch length of the other segments. Then cut it in half down through the length of it. This will give you two half flowers. Place one cut side down along the length of the larger diameter cane. Gently squeeze the other half flower into a circle again and add it to the complex cane at the joint of the other two flowers. Place the whole leaf and half-leaf sections in a pleasing sort of way around the multiple flower cluster as shown.

The next step is to fill in the indents and make the whole thing round again—something you'll want to keep in mind in your placement of the leaf pieces. It sometimes helps to draw a circle on a piece of paper that your flower and leaf cluster fits inside. This shows you the amount of "fill in" you'll be doing. Make more triangle snakes of your remaining background color and use them to fill in all the grooves until the cane is somewhat round. Try not to have any leaf or flower color showing on the outside length of the cane. This protects your points from rounding off. Lay a thin strip of background color over any other colors that are showing.

Gently press everything together, allow to rest and carefully reduce.

Square Repeat Pattern Canes

Olga Porteous showed me the trick of making square canes out of round ones. Start with two equal sections of your original cane, and more clay. This can be the same background as is used in the cane, or a totally different color that goes well with the ones you have used. Place one cane section before you, and slice down the length of the middle of the cane, making two half-circle shaped canes. Place them both flat side down on your work surface, and again cut down the length of the middle of each, making a total of four quarter wedges.

Apply each quarter section to the remaining round length of cane, with the points of the quarter sections facing outward to become the corners of the square cane. There may be a small, empty space in between each quarter section as you space them evenly around the round length. These should be filled in with small snakes of the correct length made of the other clay.

Gently squeeze the resulting square cane to slightly compress it. The cane can be reduced by carefully compressing the cane inwards, working up and down the length of the cane with even pressure of your fingers. You can also use an acrylic rod, brayer or roller down the length of each side of the cane, pressing gently into your work surface. The square cane may be further changed by cutting pieces of equal length and then stacking those pieces. This gives a repeat pattern effect where the corners meet and recombine the original flower design. You can continue to reduce, cut, and recombine pieces of square cane, or use them as they are.

For a patchwork effect, stack different square canes.

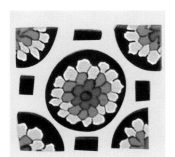

pink chrysanthemum square canes

square canes

stacked squares

The Rose Cane

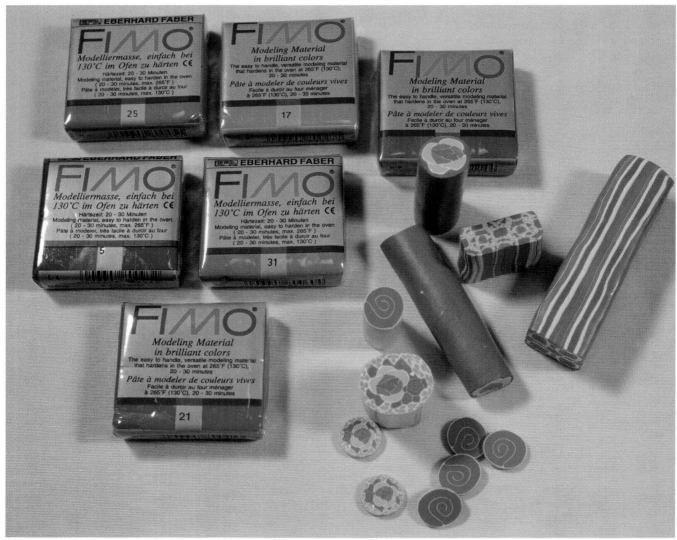

FIMO rose cane

This made a lot of cane. You can make a smaller version with less clay. You can also use different colors.

Condition the clays and mix all colors completely. Using half of the dark petal color, form a wedge about 6 inches long and a few inches across, with the thick part about 3/4 inch high and the thin part 1/4 inch or so. Place a thin layer (a #4 pasta roller setting is about 1/16 inch on my machine) of ivory on the bottom face of the wedge. I used ivory, but you can use black, or the background color of the cane if you prefer. Go for contrast.

Start at the narrow end and roll with the ivory showing outside as you go to form a jelly roll, ending with

To make the rose cane pictured here, you will need clay for the center, petals, leaves and background. In this example, I used the following colors of FIMO:

2 oz. magenta mixed with 2 oz. rosewood (dark)
4 oz. rosewood (medium)
2 oz. champagne (mix half with 2 oz. white for ivory)
2 oz. ochre
6 oz. white
1 oz. green mixed with 4 oz. dove gray and 1/2 oz. brown to make the leaf color

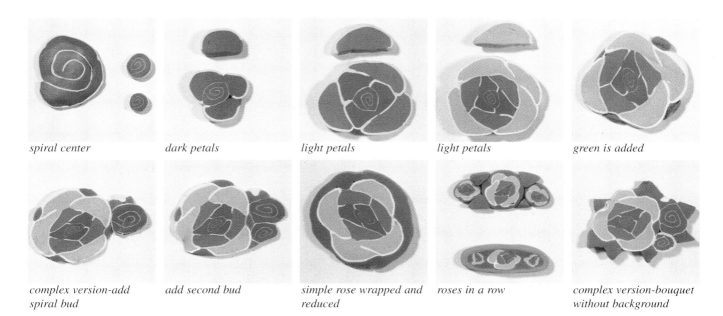

spiral center	*dark petals*	*light petals*	*light petals*	*green is added*
complex version-add spiral bud	*add second bud*	*simple rose wrapped and reduced*	*roses in a row*	*complex version-bouquet without background*

the thicker section. Reduce this to about 12 inches long, or a 3/4 inches diameter. Cut this jelly roll cane in two sections, and set one piece aside for use as a rose bud. The other will become the center of the rose. Reduce it some more to about 1/2-inch diameter.

Roll the remaining dark petal color into a 12-inch snake. Pinch the top down the length of the snake to make the center higher, more like a little mountain ridge. It should resemble a triangle snake, but not so pointy. Cover the top and sides, but not the bottom, with a #5 layer of ivory, rolled out like a tongue. This will become the dark petals. Do the same things with 4 oz. of the medium color and ivory to form the snake for medium petals. Now cut off 3/4 inch or so from both ends of the dark and medium snakes. Mix these bits with about 4 ounces of white clay to make the light petal color. Add a little more color if needed. Form into a snake and cover as with the dark and medium.

Take a section of the jelly roll center. I used one about 5 inches long. Reduce your dark petal snake by gently rolling and stretching until it is three times longer than the center segment. Cut the dark snake into three pieces and place around the center evenly as shown.

Reduce the medium petal snake and cut into three sections, placing them over the joins of the dark petals around the outside of the rose. Press all parts together towards the center very carefully to make sure that there are no air pockets and all parts are joined. Reduce very slightly, cut into two sections, with one around 5 inches long. Put the extra aside for a square cane later. Reduce the light snake and cut into four or more segments, placing them around the rose.

Roll small, green snakes and place them in the divots between the light petal segments. Fill in all the way around the rose. Carefully reduce this to about 8 inches and cut into two pieces. Cover one half with a #1 wrap of green and reduce to the diameter of your choice. This is the finished single-rose cane!

Use the other unwrapped half to build a complex bouquet. Reduce the remaining dark center bud cane that you previously set aside, and cut into two pieces the length of the remaining rose cane. Place the buds along the length of the rose and add more green snakes to pack the pieces together. Use the remaining green to form a pinched triangle snake, which is a simple leaf. Cut into sections and place them around the rose and buds cluster. Allow this to rest while you form the background.

Although a plain-colored background can easily be packed into place, this example shows a figured effect. This is done by layering the remaining ochre, champagne, and ivory clay in a stack. Trim to form a rectangle and roll into a jelly roll cane, with the white side out. Reduce the cane to a 1/2-inch diameter, cut off the final inch from each end, and mix this thoroughly with the remaining white. Cut the jelly roll into three segments, place together with snakes of the white mixture, then wrap the resulting three-spiral cane with the remaining white mixture. Reduce this cane, cut into many segments, and use it to pack around the rose bouquet cane. Pack until the cane face is mostly round again. Try to avoid having the green from the leaves showing on the outside. Wrap with a solid layer if desired (I did not on this example). Allow to rest, then reduce.

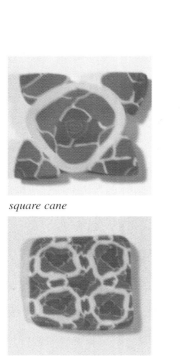

square cane

reduced

reduced

stacked

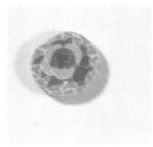

jellyroll spiral

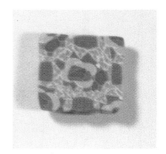

stacked

wrapped

reduced

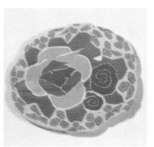

with background added

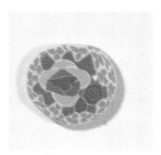

reduced

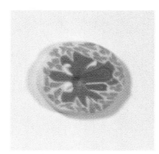

reduced

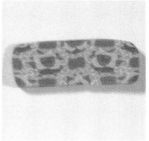

squared

reduced

secondary cane in end

squared in a row

Covering Existing Forms

things to cover

Clay can be baked all by itself, or as a covering over a form, which can be permanently a part of the final product, or used only as an internal mold and then removed. Any organic material such as rock, glass, metal, paper, cardboard, bone, wood, pottery or porcelain, and even eggshell can used. Be cautious with wood as it sometimes swells or releases moisture if not completely dried, or if it has been chemically treated.

The little wooden beads that are used in car seat covers are wonderful to cover with clay and bake. There are a lot of them in one seat cover, and many people throw them away when it begins to come apart. My sons unravel these for me and then I have an abundant source of these cores for larger polymer clay beads. They can be covered with plain clay and then impressed or otherwise decorated, or cane slices can be placed around the wooden bead. Take care to keep

car seat beads

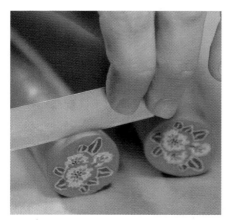

cut slices

apply slices to bead

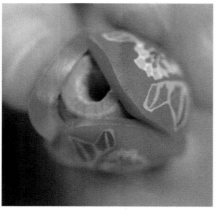

keep track of the hole

pierce from both ends

the holes visible, poking them again with a skewer if needed. The slices are then pressed together, using tiny bits of added clay if needed to close any gaps. Roll the bead in the palms of your hands in the natural curve of the palm.

Smoothing and reshaping can be done as needed to keep the bead round or make it into another shape. Pierce the bead, inserting the point of a bead reamer, needle, or wooden skewer into both the top and bottom holes. This makes both holes neat and avoids the "blowout" effect. Beads can be threaded onto a bamboo skewer and baked in pans or merely placed on paper-lined baking sheets. More ornate beads can be placed in little puffs of acrylic stuffing for support. This bakes well at recommended temperatures.

Papier-maché or cardboard jeweler's boxes also bake with ease, and can be covered to transform the simplest items into stunningly beautiful and very lightweight treasures. Rocks can be used to form little masks by laying the clay directly onto the rock and baking, then popping them off afterwards. You can cover rocks entirely and then use a utility knife to slice the clay when it is still warm from baking to form vessels with lids. Full-sized wearable masks can be

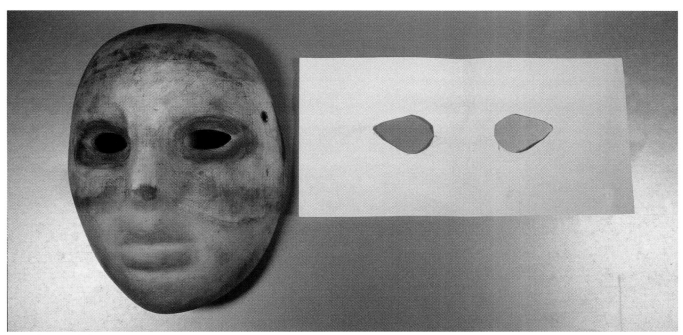

porcelain mask form, paper pattern

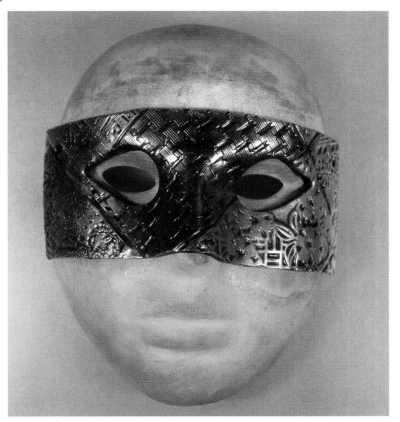

mask on form

formed over porcelain masks that are found at craft or hobby stores, or sold to be decorated with paints and ribbons and such. I use them to shape my polymer clay masks and have baked the one I have at least 50 times, popping the finished mask off after it has been baked and cooled.

Remember that earthen clays, metal, and glass have already withstood temperatures far beyond what they will endure when baking the polymer clay. Paper does not ignite until 451° F, and we don't bake at more than 300° F. Rock takes volcanic heat to change it, and eggshells are far sturdier than they look! Be sure to drain and dry them first. Blown eggs are very light-weight and can be covered with clay for collectable eggs, or the egg can be filled carefully with rice, then covered and baked to make musical shakers. I also use them as the basis for doll and puppet heads, as they are the perfect shape, and make the head much lighter and less likely to crack during baking.

Some plastics can also withstand baking. Light switch and outlet plug plates, sold in hardware stores everywhere, can be covered with polymer clay and baked. In fact, the hardware store holds a great many items that can be covered with clay. Although the clay initially sticks to the forms, you may find that they pop off with time. This can be remedied by gluing the clay to the form, using either CA super glue (cyanoacrylate), or a white PVA (polyvinylacrylate) glue such as SOBO or Aleene's Craft Glue. These can be used to glue pieces after baking or before.

I don't like the smell of baking super glue, but the PVA glues work very well, and I use my white glues to lightly coat a switch plate or other form. I let it sit a few minutes to get tacky, and then lay the raw clay on top, smoothing it gently and wiping off any excess that runs out at the edges. It bonds the form to the polymer, even as it bakes. I use it when covering jeweler's boxes made of cardstock, and it keeps the clay tight against the form, eliminating the occurrence of any bubbles.

Cornstarch is used to make some new kinds of packing "peanuts" used for filler in shipping, and it dissolves when wet. You can use these to cover with tiny strips, balls, and coils of polymer clay to make lovely filigree beads, and then remove the core after baking by placing them under running water. Do not use the other kinds of foam packaging peanuts. Styrofoam (at least the kinds available in the U.S.) melts and burns, and releases nasty fumes.

You can also use polymer clay itself as a filler or form to cover. One of the most useful ways to do this is with tube beads. We call this the "hot-dog in the bun" technique, because it looks a bit like that, and helps my students remember in which direction things go. To do this, roll out a snake as wide as your thumb, and around 10 inches long. Flatten it slightly. Cut it in half to form two 5-inch lengths. These are the "buns." Take a bamboo skewer (or length of wire, or knitting needle) and think of it as the "hotdog." Lay it on top of the bottom "bun" down the length of it and in the middle. Place the other bun on top of this. Gently pinch the seams together, with the stick still in place, and extending out at either end.

Start in the middle and gently roll the whole thing on your work surface, to meld the seams completely. Move your fingers from the middle towards the ends

as you go, but don't press too hard. You shouldn't be making grooves with your fingers, just rolling the whole thing. This may take a few attempts to get the feel of it, but should not be too difficult. If it isn't working, chances are good you started with your bun pieces too thin. Try again with thicker pieces. If the whole thing is wobbling about on your stick as you roll, or if you hear a sort of "wubba-wubba" flopping as you roll, you may have some air bubbles trapped in there. This can be corrected by pressing the clay gently in on itself, towards the stick in the center of the piece. Start at the center of it all and work towards the ends, then re-roll. You should now have a tube of clay with a stick down the center of it.

There are several ways to use these. You can decorate the unbaked tube with cane slices, placed so that they touch, or so that there are places in between where the original tube of clay still shows. Roll the whole thing to firmly affix the canes and cut into sections if desired.

Instead of decorating with canes, take a thin snake of clay and run it down the length of the tube. Hold one end of the tube in place on the stick and roll the other end forward. This will cause the whole thing to twist, and the snake will spiral around. The more you roll, the tighter the spiral. Done with a raised snake, you will get a raised spiral effect. Done with the snake rolled flat where it is stuck to the bun, you will end up with stripes. If you do this with a snake or strip that has metal foil on top, you get the effect of a metal spiral stripe. If it is done with the same color of clay in the tube and the snake, the snake "disappears" and you get the effect of a free-floating stripe of metallic!

If the original "buns" that form the tube are made of leftover ends of canes that have been chopped up and rolled into a snake, you will get lovely fine stripes of many colors, more finely placed than you could otherwise do. You can also take a stick, needle, or back of your knife to "draw" down the length of the clay, and get a "feathered" effect similar to paper marbling effects. It works by pulling the colors slightly, and works best on softer clays.

Another way to use this hot-dog and bun technique is to roll until the original tube is rather long and thin. If it is longer than your stick, you can cut it into two sections, slide one off, and insert another stick, making two of them. Trim the ends, and bake as is. Right after baking, slide the resulting tube off of the stick. It will look like a drinking straw, and you can chop it into small segments to make solid color heishi beads to use. They make great spacers.

Solid-color tubes can be textured with other tools as well. Crumpled aluminum foil works to make stone,

chop the remnants

compress

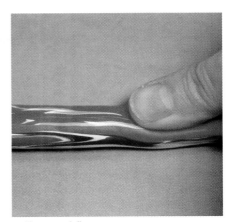

roll out and flatten

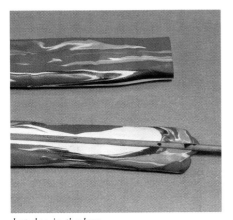

hot dog in the bun

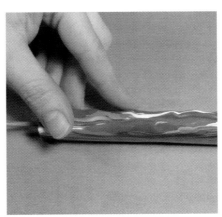

pinch seams together

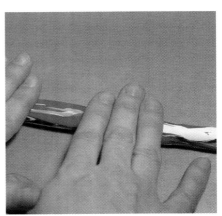

roll

apply some foil

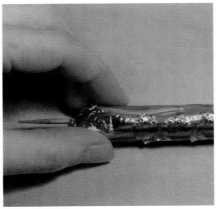

apply in one section

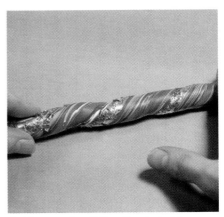

hold one end, roll the other to twist

continue to make stripes

pinch and drag

feathered effect

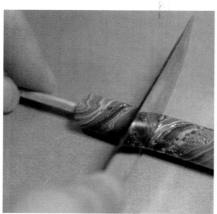
cut tube beads

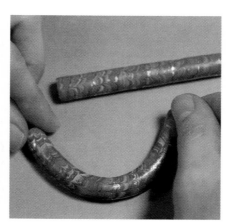
u-shaped bead

slice baked beads

bone, or coral textures, and a fine-toothed comb drawn down the length of the tube, or used like a meat tenderizer to lightly pound tiny holes, also provides an interesting effect.

Stamps can be used to transfer designs onto the tube beads. Cut them into desired lengths before applying the stamped powders or you will smear them while cutting. Rest one end of the skewer in something solid—I use my knife handle—and hold the other end, so the beads on the stick are suspended in the air above your work surface like a little bridge. Stamp along the length of the set of cut beads, then turn to stamp the other sides of the beads. Having them suspended like this allows you to reach all the sides without smearing what you have just done.

Cut tube beads can also be slipped off of the stick and placed one at a time onto a different stick, needle or bicycle spoke (available in bike stores). Holding this stick at either end of the tube bead like a tiny axle, you can then roll the bead over a stamp or texture piece, such as a matrix from Ready Stamps, flat mold you've made, or other item with a raised or indented surface,

and impress a design. It takes a bit of concentration to learn to stop when you reach the starting point again, otherwise your design is overprinted and not as clean. Don't press too hard, or the hole will become too large and may tear the bead completely. Even pressure is needed here. Place the beads back onto a skewer and bake. I usually thread six or seven at least onto a bamboo skewer.

Even if the beads still stick together a bit at the cut edges they can be easily snapped apart after baking. A single baking tray can hold dozens of skewers at a time, and I usually wait till I have a full pan or two, and then bake.

Lengths of tube beads can also be taken off the sticks before baking and bent gently to form a "U" shape. Be careful not to pinch the holes closed. Place the bead on a little nest of fiber stuffing or quilt batting—it withstands baking and protects the piece from flattening on one side. Bake as usual.

If you want to get still more bead shapes, you can thread cord or wire through an unbaked tube and bend it into odd shapes—even tie a knot. Tug the cord

apply canes to tube bead

after rolling

gently to make sure it can be removed later, and then bake. Remove cord or wire when the bead has cooled enough to harden but is still warm.

For beads with smaller holes you can use the same hot dog-and-bun technique, using a wire instead of the bamboo skewer. It is easier to perfect your skills first on the skewer version, then move to the wire, which is a bit harder to control but still useful.

To Cut Tube Beads On The Stick

Using a knife or blade held at a right angle to the raw clay, you can press through the clay to touch the stick. Roll it slightly forward, away from you on the work surface, to trim the ends evenly. You can also do this to cut beads cleanly before baking, moving along the whole thing in increments. If you hold your knife very straight and go at an even speed it will meet the

slices around a clay lump

texture solid color tubes

cut where you started, giving a nice clean edge to each bead—or if not, you get a spiral.

It takes a little practice, but is well worth it. Practice this on an undecorated tube so you don't waste any canes while you are getting the knack. Ragged-edged beads can be trimmed later if needed. You can also bake it first and then slice, but there is much more resistance with the thicker versions. You can reheat and cut while warm to make it easier.

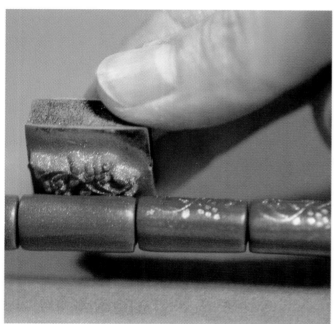

stamping cut tube beads

ponce bag and matrix board

tube bead on a stick is rolled

apply powder to raised areas

Using Findings, Glues and Joinery

barrettes are baked on the finding

Findings such as pin backs, barrettes, clasps, tie tacks, button shanks and more can now be found frequently in craft stores. More selection and price breaks on quantity purchases can be had by shopping via catalogs. Most have wholesale rates available to those customers who have obtained a sales license or resale permit (these vary by state). When you add in the shipping costs, especially for glues and other items that may be considered hazardous by postal regulations, the cost for a few things might be more than it costs to purchase locally, but quantity buys are usually well worth the time and effort to those who are making and selling their work. It's worth looking into.

Super glues work best with polymer clays. These come in many varieties. Some you need to mix, some work right out of the bottle or tube. These work by actually melting the molecular bond of the polymer and reforming it in adhesion to the metal finding. This makes for a much stronger join than can be achieved with glues that are merely sticky. Most hot glue guns use a type of glue that will not bond for more than the time it takes for the temperature to change, and it is not suitable for polymer clay. Some artists use E-6000™, or GOOP™, but my own preference is for a cyanoacrylate glue called Pic Stic™ or a glue called SuperT CA. Local hobby/model stores often carry a good selection of CA glues.

Use special caution with all chemical glues. You don't want to be splashing glue around, and use adequate ventilation. Always read the cautions on the bottle and follow instructions. I personally cannot stand the smell of E-6000, but other artists have used it with success. Be careful not to get the super glues on your fingers, and if you do get some on you, ***do not*** put your fingers together. It bonds leather and that means skin! Rather than try to wipe it off with your fingers (and gluing them together) wipe any spills onto a paper towel or rag. It is easier to scrub dried glue off of one part of you than it is to separate two parts. Scrub off any dried buildup with a coarse washcloth or scrubbing square, or use a pumice stone meant for callus removal. Washing a load of dishes or just soaking in hot soapy water helps with glue removal.

To join clay to other substances like wood, paper, fabric or glass, use a white glue that is listed as PVA. This includes SOBO™ and Aleene's™ Tacky Glue. Flecto Varathane can also be used in this way, but should not be used where great strength is required.

There is a liquid form of polymer clay called Translucent Liquid Sculpey or TLS that is used by many to join polymer to polymer, or to fill in small cracks or effect repairs. I have not used it enough to speak knowledgeably on it, but Jody Bischell has a videotape available on its use. You can find out further facts at The Clay Factory of Escondido, California.

Stringing Techniques

a pile of purple

The simplest way to string a necklace is to put a bead on a cord and tie the two ends together. Do it with a long enough cord and the resulting necklace can be placed over the head with no clasps or closures needed. Square knots tied onto leather cord are very easy and effective. There are entire books available on knots and tying, and decorative uses of cords such as macramé and oriental knot work, so if you choose, you can get very fancy indeed.

For most necklaces, simple knots will suffice. Ends can be left showing on decorative cords, or hidden by running them back through beads after knotting or by wrapping them with other threads, metal wire, or cap end findings. Most bead and hobby stores carry a selection of clasps, bails, and other findings, and these can also be ordered from the manufacturers' catalogs if you need them in large quantities. When postage is added to small wholesale orders it can be as expensive as buying retail, so patronize your local merchants when possible.

You can use very thin threads for stringing, such as NYMO, or thicker cords and fibers. You can use telephone wire, which is plastic coated. Tiger Tail is also coated with acrylic, but can still cut through the polymer clay beads if too much tension is applied, as can thin wire. SoftFlex™ wire is far more pliable, but it is also strong and does not kink like Tiger Tail. Both need crimp beads for use with clasps or a self-join, as knotting does not work well.

Thicker wire can be used to make pendant beads or

India girl bead pendants

Southwestern girl beads

not need a clasp. Use a piece of cord 1 foot longer than the desired finished length. This will give you 6 inches on either end for tying off. If your cord or thread is prone to fraying, add several more inches when cutting your length. Thread beads onto this cord in a way that pleases you. It can be symmetric, with a single focus in the middle, or not—it's up to you. To keep it from looking clunky, use small beads as spacers in between larger beads, or knot work, as is done in strands of pearls. I like to use a variety of beads, both glass and metal, as well as other kinds. I collect them and sort them into big sealable plastic bags by color. When I am ready to string I can "go shopping" through my collections to find the most pleasing combinations.

to make links with a bead in the middle. These can then be used separately or chained together.

I am very fond of using a three-ply nylon twist cord for my necklaces. It comes in colors, on cones, is thick enough to use without a needle, and thin enough that I can use several strands together for more dramatic effect, and still get several strands through single beads at the ends of necklaces.

Single-strand necklaces longer than 30 inches do

I tend to string necklaces in asymmetrical ways. I have a couple of items that make stringing much easier. One is a plastic lid to a large food storage container I got at a restaurant supply store a long while back— the groove where it fits onto the container is just right for laying out beads into a circle. When I string, I pull out everything I think I might want in that color. Tiny beads (spacers of glass, polymer or metal) go into the flat part of the center in a few jewelers box (cardboard) lids to keep them separated and yet available. Then I go through the bigger beads, usually the polymer ones and a few collected goodies in glass or whatever, and I lay them around in the groove. I start with something large in the middle, leave a little space, and then I distribute the other ones somewhat equally around the groove. This might be three tube beads on either side, with a couple of medium round ones in there, too. This is just to make sure there are enough and that I like the colors and the mix.

After this I do the actual stringing. Sometimes it's

Japanese girl beads

multi-strand face pendant necklace with Klew bead accent

easier than others. I take a string apart and redo it as many times as it takes. I tend to have a wave form in my patterns. From the center it might be biggest, medium, small, small, small, medium, medium, big, medium, small, small, small, medium, and so on. This is especially important for the ones I do with five or six strands as I want the waves to fit next to each other, so the big ones on one strand are next to the little ones on another, and so on.

I use just a little symmetry for the left and right sides, mostly in size. Biggest beads are in the center of the necklace, middle sized on the sides, and then they get smaller towards the top. I don't enjoy counting so I developed my method as a way to get them strung without having to match things perfectly. One of the other things I try not to do is put two beads that are the same next to each other, but to space them out. Doing it before the stringing helps me to do this quickly as I can play around a little with the spacing while still on the lid/bead board. I try to put tubes in between rounds and things like that, to help give some variety. Then again, I've also done necklaces with all tube beads, and small glass rounds between each. Each project is different.

When you've picked out and assorted the beads you want to use, and strung them into a necklace, finish with at least 1 inch of larger holed beads on each end. I usually use a tube bead and a round signature cane bead. The reason you want a larger holed bead and not a seed bead is so that the ends of the cord can be run back through after the knot is tied. Begin to tie a knot—pick up the necklace after the first cross-over of the cord ends, and pull to remove any hidden slack. The necklace will relax somewhat over time, and you want to begin rather tightly. Switch the knotting ends in your grip so that you are holding what was the right side with the left hand, and the left side is now in the right hand.

This half rotation will keep the tension tight as you tie the rest of the knot. Finish off the knot, and tie one more time for a doubled knot. Then thread the ends of the cord onto a large-eyed needle if needed and run the needle and thread back through the last inch or so of beads. Carefully cut off the exposed ends. By doing this an inch or two away from the knot, you make it much less likely to come apart. This also hides the raw cord ends. I use a dot of super glue or jeweler's cement at the opening of the bead hole where the cut end sits, and also on the knot itself.

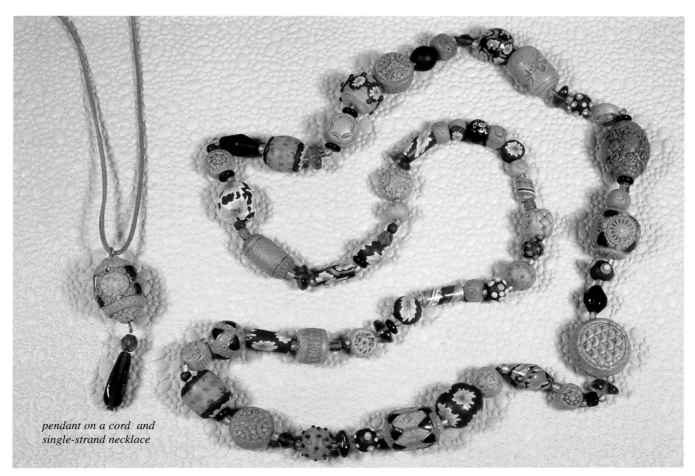

*pendant on a cord and
single-strand necklace*

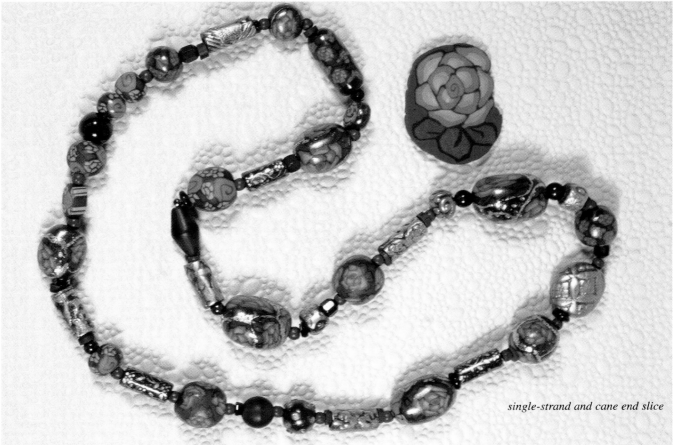

single-strand and cane end slice

Beaded Pendant and Necklace Variations

bead pendant necklace

This project includes a bead and wire pendant that can be worn quite simply on a chain, or it can be strung into a long and elegant swath of beads! The beads shown here are polymer clay, glass, and metal, but any beads can be used. The "girl beads" shown here are made with an appliqué process of many tiny slices of hand built polymer canes layered onto a polymer core. Some have been formed into pendants.

The first step to successful stringing is to gather your components. Beads that don't get used in the necklace can be used to make the coordinating project earrings. Bring out your accumulated treasures and see what goes together for your own tastes. I always enjoy going through my stash of beads and pulling out what I need. It is important to build up a good supply in order to be able to work with multiple colors and forms. You should always be on the lookout for unusual beads and pieces to add to your reserves. You never know what is going to work with a piece until you start to dig in and look. Both the thread and the wire from the piece above are available at most bead stores.

You will need
- scissors
- round-nose (chain-nose) pliers
- a large-eyed needle (crewel needle)
- jewelers cement or super glue
- chain necklace (if desired)
- beads
- 20-gauge jewelry/craft wire stringing thread
- three-ply nylon twist

To Make The Pendant:

Cut a 6-inch piece of wire. Use the tip of the round-nose pliers to curl a small loop at one end of the wire, then bend the wire slightly where the circle closes.

Thread the beads onto the wire, using small spacers in between if desired. You may need to try several arrangements and combinations until you are pleased. I have a metallic seed bead, and then the small vintage glass crystal bead, a girl bead, and another crystal bead followed by a seed bead. Trim wire if needed to about 1 1/2".

Use the wider part of the round-nose pliers to make two loops, starting down by the seed bead at the top of the large bead. Wrap the end of the wire back around the original stem, by the seed beads, under the start of the loops. Make these "carrier" loops large enough to feed your favorite delicate gold chain through, or for one or more strands of strung beads.

To Make The Necklace:

Cut your stringing cord to the desired finished necklace length plus 12 inches. I often make necklaces long enough to go over the head easily and require no clasp. Slide the pendant onto the stringing cord, centering it. Add beads in a pleasing formation on either side. You can make it strictly symmetrical or opt for a more varied look. The use of smaller spacer beads in between the larger components focuses more attention on the beads by separating them, and can be an effective way to use those special collected treasures.

When the necklace is strung to your liking, make sure that the last inch or so of beads on either side have holes large enough for the crewel needle, and for the stringing cord to go through twice. Tie a knot, making sure there is no slack in the necklace. It's best to let it dangle, but be very careful not to let it go until the knot is done. If you are satisfied with the knot placement, tie the knot one more time to double it, and then use the crewel needle to take the cord ends on either side back through the last inch or so of beads. Cut the tails of the cord close to the last beads through which they came. Be careful to avoid the bead-carrying strands. Place a very small dot of glue or jewelers cement directly on the knot and the cut thread ends to secure them. Allow it to dry before wearing.

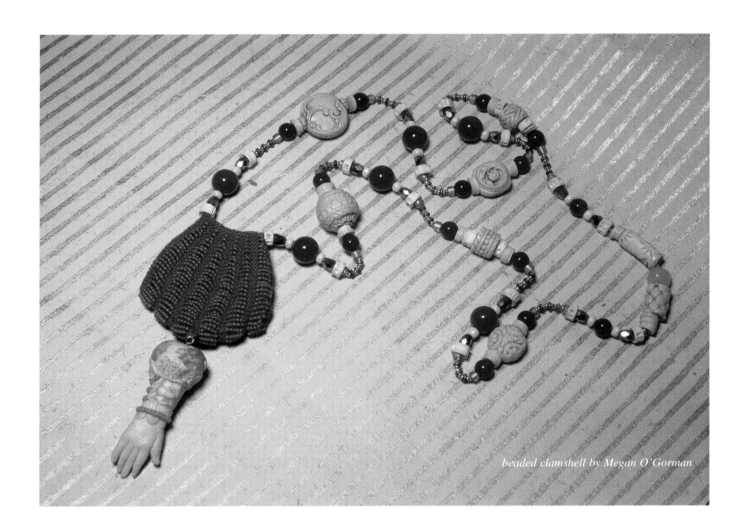

beaded clamshell by Megan O'Gorman

Sources and Resources

noh face, cobalt and gold tone necklace

Thermoplastics, or heat-set plastics, have been available for home use since the 1930s when Bakelite crafting kits were sold. Bakelite, now extremely collectable under this and several other brand names, was invented in 1907 by Leo. H. Baekland as he searched for a formula for synthetic shellac. This first form of synthetic plastic has a wide range of industrial and decorative uses. It became very popular between the 1920s and 1950s and was widely used for buttons and costume jewelry. Coco Chanel and other designers used it to fantastic fashion effect. However, it had a phenol (carbolic acid) and formaldehyde base, and it was very flammable as well as needing special precautions for its use. It also changes color with age due to the chemical reactions that take place within. A very beautiful and inspiring book titled *The Bakelite Jewelry Book*, written by Davidov and Dawes, has lots of information about the history and usage of this premier form of plastic.

The modern forms of polymer clay no longer have a phenol base and are much safer to use. When used according to the directions, they qualify as "non-toxic" under federal law. For more complete information about the chemical structure of polymer clays, I recommend Nan Roche's seminal book *The New Clay*. It is the source from which many artists creating in polymer clay have first drawn a working understanding of this wonderful medium.

Multi strand rope with tasseled pendant

items without a preconceived notion of what they are supposed to be used for, you will often find amazing tools and treasures. Get past the thought that you know what things are, and you will find far fewer limits and much more fertile territory to explore. Try looking at things with the thought "what could this have to do with my clay?" Suddenly, the garlic press becomes a small strand extruder, and the meat tenderizing tool is a texture imprinter. Cookie cutters are clay cutters. Try decorative edgings using just a bit of a cutter that has a pleasing shape. Curves and triangles can both be found in a heart-shaped cutter. Stars with points can be used to cleanly remove parts from pieces to be onlaid or appliquéd.

You can even use cookie cutters to cut thick sheets of clay into components for millefiore cane building. Candy or candle molds—both are useful for polymer clay. Metal ones can be baked. The side of that metal grater with the tiny holes was meant for lemon zest, or nutmeg—but it works wonders on old, hard clay, to turn it into tiny inclusions for translucent clays or faux turquoise and other stone looks. You can also press the clay on to it, or roll beads over it.

Decorative-edged scissors meant for fabric or paper work fine on sheets of well-conditioned clay. In fact, many tools meant for these two media have useful applications with polymer clay. Pin heads can be used in decorative ways.

Polymer clays are available in many hobby and craft stores, and through mail order from companies around the world. Tools are found in a multitude of places, from art supply stores, to kitchen and cooking supply sources, to hardware stores. Grocery stores hold a wealth of supplies and tools, including bamboo skewers for beads, parchment paper for baking and storing clays, plastic wraps, and texture tools such as aluminum foil, garlic presses, and combs meant for babies or pets. Fly swatters, shelf paper, and other items can also be used for texture, and such items as pastry decoration tools and cookie cutters can be found there as well.

When cruising the aisles as you shop, try looking at things with a fresh perspective. If you look at

cutters

Straight pins can be used in tiny sculptural armature, as can wire. Grids meant for measuring fabric can be used with clay—these are great under a sheet of clear acrylic as a work surface, giving you an instant size reference as you go. You can also put an image under these clear acrylic sheets, and use it as a pattern when building canes.

Many things in the cosmetics aisle of the store can be useful, too—everything from little baskets and containers, makeup brushes, makeup powders and pencils, containers and bottles that can be covered or decorated can be found there. Also look for textures on the backs of plastic mirrors or other such items, and in barrettes or other costume jewelry. Often these can be used to impress designs into items that are totally unlike the original piece.

The hardware store is another rich source of inspiration, form, and tools. Texture is everywhere—sandpaper, nail heads and points, screws and nuts and bolts, saw blades, plastic or metal mesh, rope and cord, overhead light panels, and much more. Lamp bases, clocks and many other items can be covered and baked, or decorated using baked clay pieces. Switch plates and plug plates add an instant decorator touch when cov-

ered and baked with clay that coordinates with the colors, texture and style motifs used elsewhere in the room. Do not, however, cover items such as lampshades or candle lanterns where the clay would be near enough to the light source to get hot.

Once you begin to look for textures, you'll find them everywhere. Many things can be used to make an interesting impression, or to make molds. Real (or artificial) leaves are used to impress clay for a natural and beautiful look brought in straight from the garden. Inspiration can be found inside, outside, and all around the town. Just keep looking. Flower and gardening catalogues, and books on floral arrangements are very useful when designing floral canes. Books on textiles, weaving, embroidery, ironwork, printing and other art forms are potent sources of design inspirations, as are books on historical designs or cultural art. Many combinations of color, pattern, and form can be replicated in your own polymer clay work.

There are also a growing number of excellent books about polymer clay, and videos are available from several sources as well. In addition, there are a number of polymer clay artists who also teach, and classes are offered throughout the United States and elsewhere in

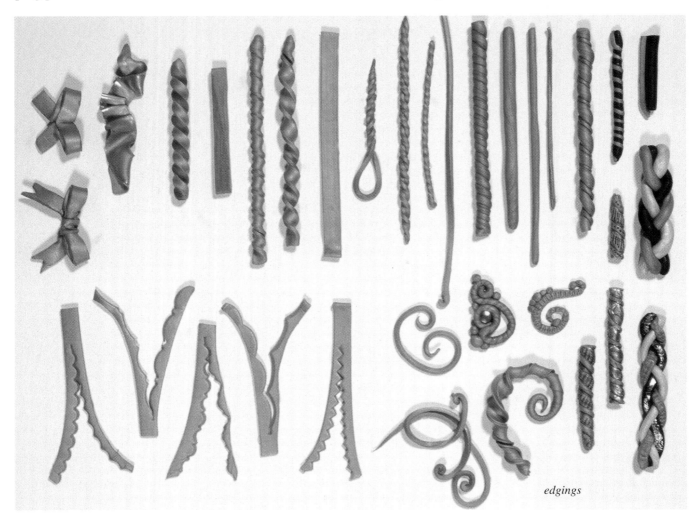

edgings

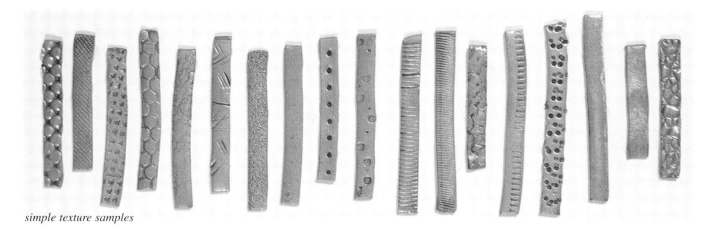

simple texture samples

the world. Conferences, retreats, trade shows, seminars and conventions are also offered every year, and there is growing availability of both the raw materials and the finished art.

There are several ways to keep in touch with what is being offered in the way of classes and events. One is to join with fellow polymer clay enthusiasts in a guild. There are many local guilds, and there is the National Polymer Clay Guild. The local guilds are independent of the national group, but efforts are made to work together to mutual advantage. It's in all of our interests to spread the word about things to do with polymer clay.

The NPCG was formed more than a decade ago to support artists and crafters and to educate the public about the use of polymer clay as an artistic medium. This is done by publicizing polymer clay work to galleries and museums as well as the public; by fostering education through sharing information, giving demonstrations and conducting workshops; and by developing opportunities for polymer clay artists to show their work to the public and to engage in public service activities.

The membership of this not-for-profit arts organization is made up of artists, teachers, hobbyists and collectors who love polymer clay. One of the chief member benefits is the quarterly newsletter *The POLY-inforMER*, which is a visual treat and filled with information.

As a member, you can rent books and videotapes from the NPCG Library, and contribute to or rent the NPCG Slide Bank, which features fascinating and historic artworks and craft projects. Members are also invited to participate in guild shows, workshops, program meetings, the National Conference held biannually, and the annual retreat in May, all at a discounted price.

All the work involved in these benefits and events is done by volunteers, and the NPCG offers its members

the opportunity to get involved on many levels. If you aren't already a member, think about joining, and if you are a member already, think about volunteering to help with the many ongoing aspects of this terrific and growing organization.

I am fortunate to have been a part of the beginnings of local guilds in two states. As a founding member of the San Diego Polymer Clay Guild, and the Colorado local guilds (we got so big we needed two), it was my privilege to be in at the start of a strong group of people with a common interest in polymer clay. I am not by nature much of a "joiner," and yet these guilds are so full of energy and bubbling with enthusiasm and great ideas for use with clay, that it was hard not to want to be a part of it all.

Many local guilds have as part of their agenda "clay days" similar to old-fashioned quilting bees, where people bring their current projects and work in a companionable furor of sight and sound. There is much show and tell, and answers for problems by those who have been there before. I have met good friends through clay days and shared many a lovely afternoon. Some of those were spent at The Clay Factory in Escondido, California, where the SDPCG holds many of its clay days.

The Clay Factory might not look like much from the outside. It is ensconced in a small agricultural town. No neon signs announce it—all the color and visual fun is inside. Howard and Marie Segal have invested decades in building this powerful little oasis for the clay world, and run it with skill and humor.

Beginning in the 1970's, Howard and Marie sold the artwork that she creates, and then the raw clay, to a growing list of artists and crafters who have found out about this wonderful media. Along with clay, powders, cutters, and other tools, Howard and Marie also supply access to the huge wealth of experience they have in using different kinds of polymer clays. Marie is a source of help and problem solving to artists with questions, in person and on the phone, and through her instructional videos. Both she and Howard are among the most supportive and informative people I have ever met in the polymer clay world. They are vendors, artists, teachers, and prominent in development of Premo Sculpey clay in conjunction with Polyform Products.

Many debts of gratitude are owed to this hardworking and often under-appreciated team. Marie's work in building the color palette of Premo clays is a valuable gift to all who use it, and yet not well known to the public. She and Howard both work endless hours to promote polymer clay and its use, and deserve more recognition and reward for that work and for all that they share freely with others. They represent much of what is finest about the polymer clay community.

The Internet is another fabulous resource to polymer clay lovers. For those who are online, there is an entire world full of like-minded people who meet regularly in cyber space to chat or leave messages about working with polymer clay, and there are literally thousands of Web sites and pages put up by artists to show their creations at any hour of the day or night.

One of the very best is Polymer Clay Central, started on the Internet by Arlene Thayer in 1995. Arlene built a place for PC artists to mix, share and learn about this emerging art form. At the time, there wasn't much on the Internet for PC. Soon, everyone was sending their links to Arlene to be listed in one of the most complete lists of PC Web sites. In 1998 Arlene transferred control of Polymer Clay Central to Leigh Ross, who was already running two very successful craft-related sites. Being both a PC artist and a forum manager, Arlene felt that Leigh would give her beloved PCC the nurturing and care she wanted for it. Together with her husband, Stephen, Leigh has maintained and improved this electronic meeting place and storehouse of information about polymer clay.

Today Polymer Clay Central is thriving, with over 250,000 Web hits a month. You'll find artist interviews, swaps, projects, monthly contests, chats, guest chats with well known PC artists, lessons, photos,

message boards and PC friends and all this is free. The URL is: www.polymerclaycentral.com.

The stated purpose for PCC is to have a safe, supportive place where all PC artists, whether beginners or seasoned professionals, can meet, share, teach and learn in a safe, respectful environment. They have a super volunteer staff that works very hard to keep everything moving in a safe and supportive manner (by the way, they are always looking for more volunteers). There are many areas of interest to explore at PCC, and more emerge all the time, making it a great place to begin surfing.

In addition to Internet Web sites, there are also several online discussion groups and news groups devoted to polymer clay enthusiasts. AOL has its own craft message areas, as do many other service providers. My personal favorite is a UseNet news group titled "Rec.Crafts.Polymer-Clay." I have been reading and posting there for several years now. There are absolute beginners and established pros that read and respond there, and it is a friendly and encouraging group of people with polymer clay as a common interest.

It is, of course, always a good idea to use proper "netiquette" when joining into discussions on any newsgroup, and this one is no exception—and do remember your posts are a matter of public record. In the newsgroup, we share information about tools, teachers, tips and some techniques, questions are asked and answered, and the combined experience and insights of the groups makes for a very large pool of information. One group member, Diane Black, has compiled, indexed, and archived years of this shared exchange and made it available at her Web site. Answers to thousands of polymer clay related questions can be found at www.glassattic.com and more is added to this great resource all the time.

My own Web site consists of more than 50 pages of information and displays of our art work, and the links and sources page I have built is an easy way to go visit hundreds of suppliers and fantastic artists. Do stop by and visit www.polyclay.com next time you are online.

Some Recommended Books:

The New Clay, Nan Roche, Flower Valley Press, Rockville, MD, 1991

Creative Clay Jewelry, Leslie Dierks, Lark Books, Ashville, NC, 1994

Creating With Polymer Clay, Steven Ford and Leslie Dierks, Lark Books, Ashville, NC, 1996

How To Make Clay Characters, Maureen Carlson, North Light Books, Cincinnati, OH, 1997

Making Miniature Flowers With Polymer Clay, Barbara Quast, North Light Books, Cincinnati OH 1998

Foundations in Polymer Clay Design, Barbara McGuire, Krause Publications, Iola, WI, 1999

The Design and Creation of Jewelry, Robert Von Neumann, Chilton Book Company, Radnor, PA, 1961, 1972

Art Nouveau Stained Glass Pattern Book, Ed Sibbett, Jr., Dover Publications, Inc., New York, NY, 1978

Plants and Flowers—1761 Illustrations for Artists and Designers, Alan Bessette and William Chapman, Dover Publications, Inc., New York, NY, 1992

Treasury of Flower Designs for Artists, Embroiderers and Craftsmen, Susan Gaber, Dover Publications, Inc., New York, NY, 1981

The Bakelite Jewelry Book, Corinne Davidov and Ginny Dawes, Abbeville Press, New York, NY, 1988

Japanese Design Motifs—4260 Illustrations of Japanese Crests Matsuya Piece Goods Store, Dover Publications, Inc., New York, NY, 1972

Art Deco Internationale, Iris Weinstein and Robert Brown, Quick Fox, New York, NY, 1977

Colette's Wedding Cakes, Colette Peters, Little, Brown, and Company, New York, NY, 1995

The Right Brain Experience, Marilee Zdenek, McGraw Hill, New York, NY, 1983

Part III

Projects

In this section, nine styles or modes of decoration will be touched upon. This is only a tiny taste of the many variations. With color mixing and an eye to detail, you can coordinate with any fabric, any design element. Any decorative treatment can be embellished!

Vintage Floral

Cabbage roses and other floral sprays bloom exuberantly on vintage textiles and again in today's reproductions. French and English "country" looks, also known as the popular "shabby chic" style, depend on these beautiful flowery patterns and colors. These glow from chintzes, bark cloth, antique lace and linens, calicos and other kinds of fabrics used together in a cohesive and cozy manner. Many original pieces can be found for sale, and textiles from the 30s, 40s, 50s and so on are very collectable now, with their value sure to grow in the coming years.

The rose cane made earlier in this book is used in this lovely display of kitchen items. The colors used to make the cane were suggested by the dusty pinks and rose, gold, ivory and blue-tinged greens in the fabric. Solid colors of clay in those tones are also used.

Here's everything a kitchen needs to coordinate and complement the look you establish with your chosen fabrics, wall and window treatments, and dishware. These touches bring it all together.

The items in this section include:

- spice jars in a set
- set of jars for beans and other dry goods
- sugar container
- oil bottle
- syrup dispenser
- bottle opener
- light switch and plug plates
- drawer pulls
- napkin rings
- beads (suitable for use as pulls at the ends of drapery or fan cords)
- vase converted from a bottle
- set of refrigerator magnets

vintage floral

Flat Applications

There are two different kinds of flat applications shown here. Some are slices of cane applied directly to items, which are then baked. It is best to warm the slices first with body heat, by holding them a minute. You can also use a heating pad set on low, covered with a tea towel and a sheet of plastic wrap, but don't go off and forget your clay or it will cook over time. There are also warmers available that use your microwave, much like gel packs for athletes. Again, care must be taken not to overheat.

Warming the slices makes them much more pliable and allows you to form them around a hard surface without cracks and breaking. This is especially important as canes get older and dryer. A well-wrapped cane, stored in the dark, will keep for several years. In this way you can build up a cane bank with a wide variety. This sort of stash is very important, as every

*finished
jar lid*

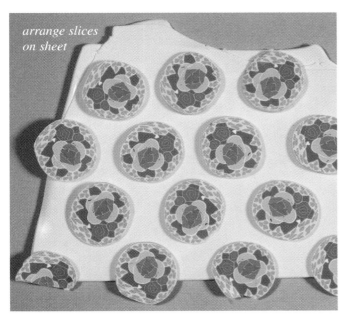

arrange slices on sheet

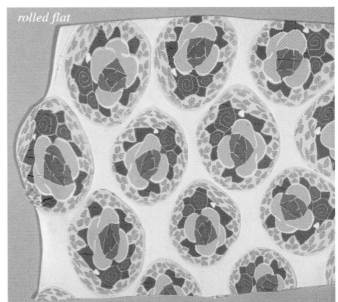

rolled flat

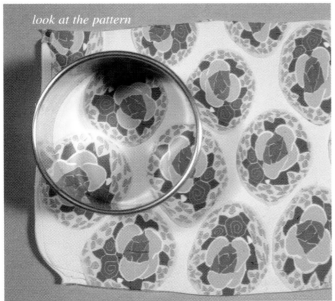

look at the pattern

cut a circle and a strip

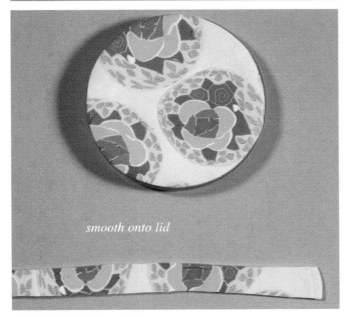

smooth onto lid

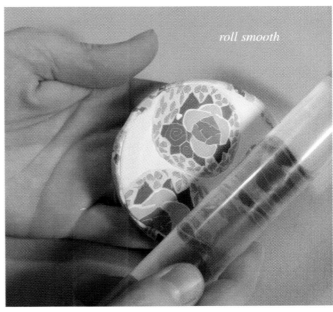

roll smooth

quilter, beader, knitter, or any other kind of artist knows. Being able to draw from a bigger variety gives you more freedom of choice.

The second flat covering technique involves making a flat sheet much like fabric, and then cutting and piecing it. The flat sheets can be decorated in many ways—by the color and texture of the clay alone, with inclusions in the clay like metallic foils, graphite flakes or micro-glitter, by impressing or stamping, or by use of cane slices. Begin with a rolled-out sheet of clay. This example shows a sheet of ivory at a #1 Atlas setting (about 1/8 inch thick).

Thin slices of cane can be cut and applied in a regular repeating pattern. They can be staggered or clustered in other ways. Look at fabric and the way it repeats for inspiration, or just do what pleases you. Press the slices evenly into the clay and use an acrylic rod, roller or brayer to evenly flatten the canes. This helps avoid a lot of distortion when you put it back through the pasta roller. If you don't have a pasta roller, then all rolling must be done by hand. It truly helps to have a machine. Sometimes the right tools make all the difference.

Once the canes are nicely in place, put the whole piece through the pasta roller at the same setting, then again at #3. If your designs have spread too much on the first pass through, your slices need to be thinner to start with. This comes with practice. Fix this by turning the sheet before the next setting. This allows the compression to go in the opposite direction. You want to end up with a #3 or #4 setting (about 1/16 inch) sheet. This is a good depth for covering sheets, in that it is thick enough not to be too stretchy and have a little depth and still thin enough not to look bulky or develop bubbles or cracks in baking. This problem is much less likely with the firmer clays and with complete preparation of any clay.

Lids

To cover jar lids of all sorts, start with clean, dry, glass jars with metal lids. Some hard-plastic lids can be baked as well. Use caution and test one before doing a whole batch. Prep the lids for best results by coating them lightly and evenly with a thin layer of white PVA craft glue, such as SOBO™ or Aleene's™. Do the top of the lid and the lip (sides) as well. Allow this to get tacky before applying the clay. It can even be completely dry and still be effective in making a good contact bond between the lid and the jar.

I cut easy and even circles by using a set of graduated circle cutters, but you can also use a utility knife or other kind of cutter. If you are covering many similar lids in this way, you can make a cardstock pattern.

However, an open cutter allows you to center the design to your liking. Many cookie and canapé cutters offer exciting clay uses.

Cut a circle the size of your lid. Measure your lid and a cut a rectangular strip as wide as the lip of the jar, and as long as the lid is around. I usually cut it extra long and find the right length as I wrap it around. After cutting it way too short once or twice you'll come to know the right approximate size fairly easily! Carefully slide a knife underneath if needed to release the clay from the work surface, rather than pull it to the point of stretching. Place the clay circle on top of the lid and smooth it lightly into place with your finger tip. Then place the rectangular strip around the lip, pulling just slightly as you go. Cut away any excess at the seam and use your finger or a rubber blending tool to smooth it together, using feathery strokes first in one direction, then back in the other direction.

Use your knife with the blade held flat to the lip bottom to trim away any excess if needed. Use your finger and thumb to meld the seam of the top and the lip. I use my thumb to lightly press the clay up towards the top, and then my finger to press the top edge into the seam, and to smooth it. Use a petting stroke with your finger to help get rid of any finger prints. Then use a roller to further smooth it a bit. Bake according to package directions.

Large and small lids—lids of an amazing range— can be covered using these simple steps. The lids of a store-bought set of spices in a metal rack were covered in this way, and the handle of the rack was covered as well. This is done by making a long, tube bead around a thick, bamboo skewer or thin dowel rod, and then slicing the bead all the way down to the skewer and down the entire length. This is done while the bead is still warm as it cuts with less resistance then. Leave the skewer in so as not to accidentally cut the beads into two halves, then remove the skewer and use the opening to fit the tube over the wire handle of the rack. I then sealed mine shut with a line of super glue and used a thin, pre-baked sheet of ivory (#5) to cut a long, lacy strip by using decorative-edged scissors. This piece is a lot like firm but very flexible ric-rac, and I just glued it in place. You could cover any of the metal parts of the rack, smooth the edges, and bake the whole thing in a larger oven.

Drawer Pulls

This same top and sides covering technique can be used with drawer pulls in exactly the same way. Use wooden, metal, glass, or porcelain knobs as these can be baked. You can paint exposed parts of knobs and decorate with a single slice of cane pressed into place,

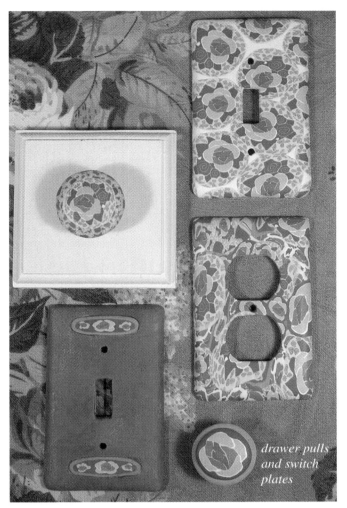

drawer pulls and switch plates

which is very much in keeping with the country look.

Notice that the rose designs used in the clay are much simpler than the cabbage roses in the fabric, but use the same coloration. This is an example of "goes with" rather than "matches." If there is a little variety, things stand out in a more individual way, and yet still harmonize. If you want a cabbage rose cane, many more layers of flattened petals must be added during the cane building.

Magnets

Use decorative cutters with leftover areas of sheets of decorated clay and bake the pieces, along with some cane slices, then glue magnets to the backs. Flat sheets of magnets found in hobby or office supply stores can be cut with scissors and glued in place. Use super glue; the sticky adhesive on the backs of most magnet sheets is not sufficient.

Bottle Opener

Cut a rectangular piece and press it into place on a "church key" bottle opener. This one has a magnet on the back as well. Repeated or prolonged baking weakens magnets, so only bake a magnetic opener like this for 25 minutes. I used a little super glue to adhere the

or cover them completely just like the jar lids. Of course, remove them from the drawer first! Many metal drawer and door pulls that are not circular can also be covered and baked.

Switch and Plug Plates

The switch plate and plug plates have been covered with sheets of clay as well. Of the three shown here, one is covered with the staggered design as shown in the lids project. Another has a closer design made with the slices placed touching each other in the initial layout, which leaves little or no solid background areas showing through. The third has been covered in a solid, teal-green sheet that was textured with sandpaper pressed into the clay after it was placed on the cover.

Slices of other complex cane made with the roses are used as a decoration. Just a few slices placed well can be beautiful, and a nice change from all-over figured patterns. After baking, the solid teal area was stained with white acrylic paint, which was immediately wiped from the surface. What stays in the little crevasses gives a whitewashed or pickled paint effect,

magnets, opener, drawer pulls and beads

clay to the metal before baking. Always use plenty of ventilation when baking.

Large beads can also be used as "pulls" on draperies, ceiling fans or lights.

Vase

Strips of clay and cane slices, some cut in half to form a flat edge, decorate the bottom and neck of a bottle, transforming it into a vase for a spray of silk flowers. These were pressed onto the bottle, smoothed and baked.

Polymer clay should be kept away from actual food contact. Cane slices applied to the outside of glass jars and containers are fine, and can be baked directly on the glass or metal. The single slice on the syrup container ties it in with the decorative theme, but keeps the clay away from the opening and away from contact with the syrup. The sugar lid is covered to the edge of the opening, but sugar is dry and there is no real contact. It is also best to cover pieces that will not be washed and immersed daily—so don't cover the

silverware. Polymer clay can easily be wiped clean with a damp cloth. In addition to avoiding direct contact with food or drink, avoid putting clay on surfaces that are heated, such as pot handles or trivets. I did, however, make some very nice replacement feet for my crock-pot when one broke.

Napkin Rings

Make napkin rings by cutting a rectangle strip of clay and forming it around a cardboard tube, such as those in paper towels or wrapping paper. Wrap the tube in a piece of paper or aluminum foil first to ensure easy release of the baked rings. Blend the seam together at the join and decorate with a cane slice, or use rubber stamps. You can also impress the clay strip while it's still flat, and then use powders to highlight the raised portions. Be sure to smooth the seam before adding the powder. Bake according to instructions. Powders must be sealed with a finish such as Flecto Varathane.

jars, napkin rings

Victorian Roses

A major characteristic of Victorian styling is the ornamentation. It was the usual thing to add not just a ruffle, but one with a lace edge, and beaded top, with ribbon inserts. And not just one, but rows of them. Every aspect has many decorative details in its finish.

The same dusty pinks, sage and soft greens, and ivory used in the previous projects are found in the charming boudoir items shown here. This look is lacier and even more feminine than the roses used in the kitchen, which can also be seen used in some accent touches here. More ivory, white and translucent clays are used in flat sheets and in canes. Canes made entirely of these shades of white look very much like lace when baked. Simple canes of pinched stripes, or bull's-eye and spiral canes, are really quite effective. Some of these can be seen on the round box lid and the vase, as well as around the candlesticks. Slices can be used to form sheets as before, or applied directly as elements to build up looks reminiscent of fancy edgings or frosting.

These same flourishes are often found in Victorian woodwork, and referred to as "gingerbread." Tiny balls of rolled clay, or twisted strips or strands, can also be used to tie these sliced elements together into a strong, cohesive, yet delicate embellishment.

Victorian roses

The items in this section include:

- ✁ jewelry chest with a carved lid
- ✁ round and square rose boxes
- ✁ candlesticks
- ✁ mini armoire
- ✁ an inlaid tile tray
- ✁ several perfume bottles
- ✁ converted bottle vase
- ✁ switch and plug plates
- ✁ drawer pulls
- ✁ earrings and buttons
- ✁ pins and barrettes
- ✁ lots of beads, including a large one used as a tie back for the curtain. With its elegant gloss finish and silky tassel, it is hard to believe it was formed over a blown-out eggshell.

Many of these beautiful objects started as plain, unfinished wooden forms bought at the local hobby supply store. It is often possible to pick these up on sale, or to use discounted "seconds" that have a blemished appearance. Most times a blemish is covered with paint or clay in the finished piece. Yard sales and flea markets, antique stalls and friends cleaning house are also great places to look for items that can be totally transformed using paint and clay.

The wooden items can often be baked right in the oven, even after painting. Baked polymer pieces can be glued into place on items you do not wish to bake. When using unfinished wood, try to look for clean, dry pieces without a lot of glue showing anywhere, as this might melt. Most pieces are already sanded and largely smooth, but could still benefit from a light sanding just to catch any rough spots.

In this set, the tray, candlesticks, round box and jewelry chest all started as unfinished wooden pieces. The tray was part of a set of three. The other two are shown later in the Art Deco and Oriental styles. All are very different, though they start out the same shape and are all painted and then tiled with polymer clay.

After sanding, all items were wiped with a cloth to remove any dust and painted with several coats of acrylic paint. I mix my own with colored acrylic paints from tubes and Flecto Varathane. This not only gives me total color mixing control, but the Flecto seals the wood and gives a nice, strong finish. It can also withstand being baked. I mix it up in baby-food jars and apply, allowing each coat to dry for an hour or two before applying another.

The more coats of paint, the nicer the finish, although you can also go for a stained or pickled-wood look by using only one or two coats and allowing wood grain to show. This kind of effect should then be covered by a coat of clear Varathane to protect the finish. You can also use it as a top coat over the final paint coat if you want more gloss. Allow all layers to dry before applying the next.

Candlesticks

These wooden candlesticks were given two coats of paint mixed with a Flecto Varathane base, an inch-long squeeze of pearl-white acrylic paint, and a very small amount of green and black acrylic paint. Many Victorian and vintage colors are "saddened," or darkened, with a bit of brown or black added to the mix. After painting, the candlesticks were decorated with thin slices of triangular lace canes. A narrow bead of white glue was painted onto the wood at the neck and the base and the cane slices were pressed onto the candlesticks there, with tiny balls of clay pressed into place at the corner joins. Both candlesticks were then laid onto a paper-covered baking tray, and baked for 25 minutes.

One candlestick was left this way, another was further decorated with ribbon, beads and a rose formed with polymer clay. It was hand built in the same way that gum paste or frosting roses are made for cakes, beginning with a rolled up spiral that is pinched together at the bottom and open at the top. Petals are made of flattened balls of clay pressed into the bottom of the flower and added around in layers. Leaves are green circles flattened and pointed on one end. Veins can be scored in with a fingernail, knife blade, or rubber stamp. Shells can also add a veined texture to pressed-clay pieces. After the flower and leaves were formed, a hole was pierced through the back of the rose and leaf piece, and when baked and cooled it was sewn into place on top of the tied pink ribbon. Additional pearl beads were strung onto NYMO thread and sewn around the neck of the candlestick. Chain and pearl bead sections taken from a piece of costume jewelry were stitched into place by the knot as a final touch of opulence.

Rose and other flower construction is also detailed in books like *Making Miniature Flowers With Polymer Clay* and *Creative Clay Jewelry* as well as several published by Wilton and others on cake decoration.

candlesticks

Round and Square Rose Box

The round wooden "shaker" style box was also unfinished and purchased at the hobby store. The bottom wood section was painted with the same light pearly green as the candlesticks, and the wooden lid was covered with sheets of clay decorated with white, translucent and ivory cane slices. This is done just like the jar lids, but a plain ivory rectangle strip used for the side. A rubber stamp was then used to impress little roses with leaves all the way around the bottom of the side. Next came an added layer of cane slices at the top seam. These are placed all the way around like lace edging, and tiny balls of clay are added at the join of each. A small piece of white clay pressed into another rubber stamp several times gives the appearance of a small lace doily, and thin strips of ivory clay that have been edged in gold PearlEx Powder and then rolled out to a #6 setting imitate silk ribbons. A notch in the ends helps further this illusion. These are placed together with several roses, both buds and full blooms, and placed to one side of the lid. All are pressed well into place, and then baked. After baking, the sides

were stained lightly with a mix of Flecto and acrylic paints. This brings up the detail in the impressed designs and gives it a slightly antique look.

The square box began as simple brown card/paper box both the top and bottom sections were covered in clay. You can cut a top and sides (only square this time) just as is done with the lids, or you can use a larger square piece with the corners cut out to form flaps. Make a paper pattern first by tracing around the box lid, then adding the width of the box sides all around. When folded down over the lid, the notched corners come together to meet at the sides. Smooth each seam well, or add another decorative piece to cover the join. This example has the box bottom covered in ivory and the top in a pearly pink. This was then decorated around the lid with a rose stamp impressed on the sides and a fan and flower stamp with gold powder on the top corners. A little spray of polymer clay roses and leaves graces the center of this dainty box. After baking, the top and bottom were lightly stained.

beads, boxes and more

round box, armoire, and bottles

Switch and Plug Plates

Some of the plates were covered using a medley of lace cane slices formed into a sheet as previously discussed. As an added touch, triangles of clay were pressed into a rubber stamp and used at the top and bottom of the plate like lace points. Tiny balls of clay at each corner add to the lace look, and after baking these areas are lightly stained and the entire plate is buffed with a cloth. In another more formal example, some rose cane slices are laid in a stripe down one side of a sheet of ivory clay. The ivory section only (not the cane part) is then pressed into a texture agent (I used a piece of plastic lace place mat, which a rose pattern). After applying the sheet to the switch plate, stamps and gold powder are used along the edges of the cane section, making it look like a gold-edged tapestry ribbon applied to lace. After baking, this plate is lightly stained to bring out the lace pattern, and a coat of Flecto is painted over the stamped gold areas to seal them. I left the majority of the cane area matte, but you can glaze the whole cane area if desired.

Armoire

This miniature storehouse for your treasures could be made into a little icon or folk type shrine, or a place to keep everything from delicate hankies to jewelry. I left the top unpainted. The first three coats of paint were ivory, and then a coat of special crackle medium was applied. After it dried, a coat of light green was sponged over the top, and it crackled as it dried, showing the lighter paint underneath. After this dried, the finish was antiqued using the Flecto stain. Only then was it ready to apply clay.

A flat sheet of ivory clay at a #3 setting (between 1/16 and 1/8 of an inch) was rolled out and impressed using the lacy place mat, and cut to fit the top of the armoire. Though baked as a flat rectangle, the clay is very pliable when warm, and I glued it to the top of the wooden armoire with white glue just a few minutes after removing it from the oven after baking. I used strips of cloth to wrap the whole armoire to hold the top firmly in place as it dried. After it dries and is unwrapped, stain is used to bring out the lace detail.

I used ivory clay to form decorative pieces, again using rubber stamps and molds to make some components, and drawing some from my pile of pieces that are awaiting the right project. The door handles were made in molds like buttons, then eased to fit around the round wooden handles like lace caps while still raw. They were carefully removed, baked, and then glued into place.

More roses were formed, along with polymer ribbons and lace as described for the boxes. After baking, these were strategically placed on top of the armoire roof and glued firmly in place with super glue (used to bond polymer to polymer or polymer to metal). A strip of baked ivory clay cut with scalloped edged scissors is used to cover the join between the polymer roof plate and the wooden armoire—it looks a bit like the gingerbread trim used in Victorian styles.

The other decorative items, including polymer cabochons, squares, triangles, and antique pearl buttons and beads, are first baked and stained and then glued into place with white glue. Carpenters' glue can also be used when gluing polymer to wood, or to fabric/fiber. Do each side of the armoire and allow to dry; it is easier to get correct placement if you don't do the whole thing at once—the glue can allow pieces to drift if you are not careful. Build up the design to your liking. The inside can be lined with decorative paper or cloth, or painted.

armoire

Jewelry Chest

The bottom and parts of the top of this chest were painted solid green, with no crackle effect. Variety actually helps to tie together a look in the Victorian styles, along with lots of detail.

The top was made as a transfer onto a sheet of ivory clay, which was first impressed with some lace around the edges. The copy was laid onto the flat area, left to sit, then baked. This transfer did not "take" well, being a copy from a machine with different, less effective toner. The faint lines were enough for a guide to carv-ing, however, so I used a carving tool to remove portions of the baked clay sheet, which is quite soft by comparison to linoleum blocks or wood. After carving, I cut all around the edges with decorative edged scissors and stained the piece, making sure all the carved lines were nicely filled with stain. After it dried completely, the carved sheet was warmed again in the oven for pliability, then glued to the top of the chest in the same manner as the armoire.

rose transfer, carved box lid, impression

Tray

The unfinished wooden tray was painted on the outside in the same steps as the armoire. The resulting antiqued green crackle effect is lovely and covers a lot of area with a pleasing color and texture. It complements the detail in the polymer nicely. The interior walls of the tray were painted a muted gold, as were the insides of the handles. The tops of the handles were painted a solid soft green without the crackle effect. When the many coats of paint were dry, the exterior of the tray was given several coats of Flecto Varathane. Then it was time for the polymer fun.

I began with a print in a Dover book titled Plants and Flowers with an illustration called *"Queen's Scarlet Garden Rose,"* though the print is in black and white. I made several copies. One was used to transfer the picture onto ivory-colored clay. The trick is to start with a good copy, firmly burnish it into place face down on the clay and let it rest for a while. After an hour or so, I baked it with the paper still in place, then peeled the paper away when it was done baking. The result was a fine reproduction of black lines against the creamy tones of the clay. After cooling, I colored the picture on the clay with Berol Prismacolor markers. I used several colors—lime green, cherry red, peach, and others—and took my time, building up washes of colors. Do not use the color blender pen, as this tends to react with the clay and the inks.

The colored plate was then trimmed to a rectangle. I drew from my supply of square tiles and made more as needed—these are 3/4-inch tiles made from sheets of clay rolled out to a #3 pasta setting and cut with a square Kemper cutter. I often use any leftover bits of rolled-out clay to stamp out some of these tiles. As long as it is rolled out, why not make a few for the pile! Then I have an assortment from which to choose. This tray uses tiles of many different shades of ivory, soft green, and a few pinks. All were baked and stained if needed.

I assembled the tray much like a jigsaw or quilt pattern. Playing with the different combinations was a lot of fun. I started with the 3/4-inch squares and worked in towards the colored transfer plate. As there was a lot of space to fill, I made a paper pattern and rolled out a larger rectangle of ivory and textured it using stamps. Then I placed the colored and baked transfer on top of it and used a razor knife to cut around the transfer plate. This clay was removed, leaving a hole for the transfer, which was then put in place and the whole piece then baked. After it cooled, the stamped ivory surround was stained lightly.

All the pieces were taken out of the tray, and a generous layer of white glue painted onto the bottom of the tray. I used a 1-inch brush and made sure it was even all over the bottom of the tray. Starting at the edges and working in, all tiles were put into place and checked that they were snug against the sides. I worked towards the middle, and placed the transfer assembly there. Due to shift, there was a little gap in some places, so I trimmed the edges a tiny bit more and made it a 1/8-inch gap all around, which I then quickly filled in with some green tiles that were cut to fit. After the extra glue was removed, the tiles were topped with a clean layer of paper and several heavy books, then allowed to dry overnight.

The final step involved a dozen or so generous coats of Flecto Varathane over the surface of the tiles, making sure all cracks and gaps were filled completely, like grout, but that the Flecto Varathane did not build up or pool on the surface of the tiles. Care must be taken to allow each coat to dry for several hours before applying the next.

Perfume Bottles

Plain glass vials from a perfume oil supplier or other source can be totally transformed with a little clay. You would never know they started with unadorned black or silver plastic tops, which were then covered with small amounts of polymer clay, just as the jar lids were done. These have taller sides, but the concept is the same. The best way to get a lovely top for these is to use a mold to make a button like piece, a cabochon, and bake it before use in the bottle top. Or you can use another sort of piece—like a pearl, other bead or crystal, and include it. Just be sure it can withstand 270° F. When covering a top like this, start with a little wad of clay on the top to affix and pad the cabochon piece. Since the cabochon is already hardened, you can touch it while melding the side wall piece to the top without distorting the design. Add little bits to help further adhere the parts, like thin slices of canes, or twists of clay, or little balls. Impressed sections can added for further details. After baking, stain or glaze as needed.

boxes, bottles, and tray

square box and bottles on tray

Antique Ivory

Many people forget that the Victorian English Era and the American Wild West coexisted in history. The Western version of the highly decorative styles of the times can be a little more relaxed, and a bit less flowery and feminine than its European counterpart. Using the ivory gold and green color palette that was seen in the previous sections, these items are finished with a bit less frippery and are stained just a step darker than the previous sets. This adds to the "antique" appearance. The switch plates and drawer pulls done in this way give the look of old lace, and add to the ambience without making a big color impact. The perfume bottles are all done in faux ivory and green this time, with no touches of white and pink.

antique ivory

The items in this section include:
- sewing box
- needle case and thimble set
- pin box
- other boxes and containers
- switch and plug plates
- drawer pulls
- buttons
- banjo
- bottles
- faux ivory beads, including bonnet head and hand beads

The banjo is an inherited piece that has been in the family for generations. Bryan encrusted it with baked cane slices in white and ivory tones, with pearls, mother of pearl rounds, and antique pearl buttons. It is very reminiscent of an old fad in England where people known as "Pearlies" embellished every visible inch of their costumes with pearl buttons in an amazing collage. We call this one "The Mother of (Minnie) Pearl Banjo."

Mother of (Minnie)
Pearl Banjo

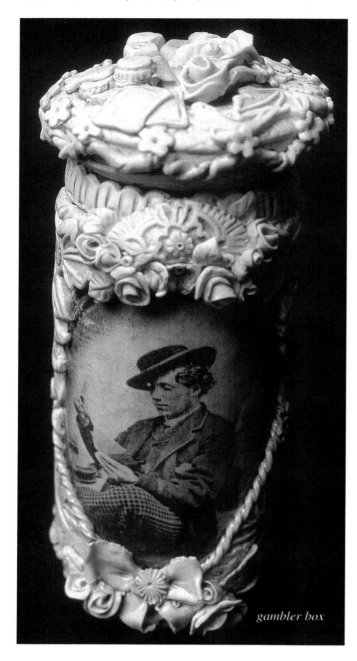

gambler box

Transfer Boxes

Start with the photocopy. I have used pictures from the National Archives of Wild Bill Hickok and Buffalo Bill. Place the copy face down on a piece of clay that has been conditioned and rolled out flat, and placed in the baking pan on the sheet of paper. Using your finger, burnish the copy onto the clay so that all the surface is touching. Let this sit for 15 minutes, then bake the clay with the copy still on top. Bake at 270° F, or according to package directions, for 15 minutes. Remove from oven and peel the copy off of the clay, disposing of the copy. The copy inks will have transferred to the clay. Trim the resulting medallion using craft scissors.

You will need:
- rubber stamps
- Band-Aid box, or other box,
- pliers
- paintbrush (plastic bristles
    —not the good watercolor brushes)
- utility knife
- pasta roller or brayer
- craft scissors
- Flecto Varathane (available in hardware stores)
- black acrylic paint
- antique gold PearlEx powder OR
    gold metallic acrylic paint
- white PVA glue such as SOBO or
    Eileen's tacky glue
- polymer clay (we used a custom color mix of
    PREMO white, translucent, and ecru)
- scrap clay
- talcum powder
- oven
- baking pan, lined with white paper
- clean rag (old T-shirt) for use in staining
- black and white photocopy of old picture

Remove the lid from the Band-Aid box using pliers (you can leave it on and cover it if you like), or use another kind of box. Coat the outside of the box with glue and allow to almost dry. It's still OK if it dries all the way. The glue helps you get the clay to stick nicely to the box.

Roll out a larger piece of clay big enough to cover the box. Start in the middle of the front and apply the sheet of raw clay, being careful to work out any air bubbles. Trim the clay so that the seam in the front meets but does not overlap. Most of this area will be covered or removed. Smooth the seam lightly with your fingertip or a brayer. Trim the top and bottom edges with the knife.

Place the cooled photo medallion onto the front of the box, wherever you find it looks good. Use the EXacto™ knife to lightly cut around the medallion, lift it up, and remove the piece you have just cut. Replace the medallion so that it is now more flush with the box covering. Wipe off any glue on the cut piece, and reuse the clay as needed for trim.

Use your fingers or a brayer to smooth the box and remove fingerprints. If the texture is still rough, you can imprint even more texture to disguise this using rubber stamps or other texture sources, such as cloth or sandpaper. You can also use stamps to impress designs into the surface, or to stamp designs onto it using stamp ink or PearlEx™ powders.

You can also use the stamps as molds, or to make molds. Lightly powder the stamps and press small, shaped pieces of clay onto the rubber stamps themselves, and use the resulting pieces to decorate your

transfer boxes

box. Trim these pulled pieces as needed for clean edges. You can use the knife, or small cookie cutters often have useful edges for "biting" away at the excess. Use these pulled pieces to cover raw edges and frame the photo transfer. Add more clay to pull the look together—tiny balls, curlicues, and ribbons or flowers formed of clay are very nice. You can also cut strips of clay, stamp them with designs, and use them as edging at the top or bottom of the box if desired. Raw clay sticks to itself with no need for further glue, just be sure to press it lightly to affix.

When you have decorated the box to your own liking, bake it according to package directions. After the piece has baked and cooled, use a little Flecto Varathane™ to paint over and seal any areas where powders or inks were stamped. Allow it to dry before further staining the box.

Mix a stain for antiquing the box using a quarter cup or so of the Flecto Varathane™, and a small amount of black acrylic paint and gold paint or powder. Mix well using the paintbrush. I use old yogurt containers or baby food jars for the stains, and mix up fresh batches as needed. Then use the paintbrush to scrub the stain mix onto the box. Do a small section at a time, and get it into all the nooks and crannies. Right away, wipe the surface firmly with the old T-shirt or rag to remove excess stain, leaving it only in the recesses. If you wipe off too much, repeat until it looks good. Do this all over the box. When it's dry, buff the box lightly using clean rags, old jeans, or a muslin buffing wheel. You can also line the box with paper if desired.

The columnar container decorated with gambler's tokens was formed around a cardboard tube. The transfer was made in the round as well, with the paper held in place by an elastic bandage wrapped around the whole thing.

faux ivory notions

Sewing Box

The wooden sewing box was first prepared with many coats of cream paint and Flecto Varathane. The decorative pieces were gathered, including some antique buttons and pearl beads, and polymer clay buttons and beads. One hand, dressed in a Victorian style sleeve, is a particularly appropriate item for this collection, and represents the high value placed on "handwork." All pieces were fixed into place, using white glue for wood-to-polymer adhesion, and super glue for polymer-to-polymer adhesion.

A wooden needle case and a metal thimble were each covered with clay to make them a part of the ensemble. This was done much like the jar lids and boxes. When dry, this box can hold lace and ribbon, or buttons made from polymer clay. With an added button back finding, cane slices and molded cabochons make fabulous lightweight buttons. You can also add earring findings or a pin back and make matching jewelry.

sewing box in pieces

glued in place

Beads

Beads made with faux ivory can be worn with many old-fashioned or retro fabric prints, and with any solid color as well. Reminiscent of Japanese Netsuke or Victorian Memento Mori, these tiny hands and heads looked carved, but are hand formed in many steps, using impressions and other techniques. Each is different, and each little head shows a unique millinery style, from a wide historical perspective. Details make each one highly individual.

Faux ivory beads strung with green glass and faux jade beads, made with more polymer clay, combine in this necklace that features multiple strands of beads twisted into a rope, and a pendant bead with a center tile of celadon green made with an oriental stamp from Uptown Design, as are some of the others in this book. All designs were used here with their permission. Some of my own designs used here are licensed and available through them as well.

bonnet head beads

faux ivory buttons

beads and bottles

bonnet head necklace

Sea Treasures

The ocean provided the shipping trade routes that supplied the world with many rare and beautiful items from far-flung cultures. Sailors brought back natural wonders that wash up on shore, such as driftwood, shells, bits of glass and even coral, as well as items from the bazaars of foreign lands. They brought back a taste for bright colors and native influences in art as well.

sea treasures

The items in this section include:
- mermaid
- switch and plug plates
- drawer pulls
- faux shell and faux coral necklace and earrings
- treasure box
- buttons
- perfume bottles

Mermaid

Mermaid

The siren shown here would be right at home on a bookshelf filled with nautical tales, or a sextant and shells. With a map or two on the wall and colorful island print fabric, a room could easily recall tropical breezes no matter how far away the sea.

The shells here are all made of polymer clay, as is the coral. Even the mermaid's scales are each hand cut from polymer clay and put in place. They are punched from a sheet of blue and silver mokume gane-style clay, using circular Kemper cutters, then each is sliced in half and applied to a layer of clay on the tail section. Her head is polymer clay formed over a blown egg, making it very lightweight. Her hair is made of hand-dyed wool roving, and her necklace is strung with seven strands of tiny polymer shells and faux coral mixed with crystal seed beads. It took almost as long to make the shells, coral and necklace itself as it did to make the mermaid!

faux shells and faux coral

Faux Shells and Coral

To make the shells and coral you will need polymer clays in the following colors:

- two small blocks white
- one small block golden yellow
- one small block red
- small amounts of black and brown, or small amounts of blue, purple or green— not much is needed. (shells come in many colors, so you can pick your favorites here)
- metallic powder, such as PearlEx powder or FIMO bronze pulver (I used gold)

And the following tools:

- small paintbrush
- jar lid
- knife or blade
- talcum powder or cornstarch
- toothpick or needle for poking holes
- piece of aluminum foil
- small piece of lightly crumpled, heavy-grit sandpaper
- two or three real seashells, preferably with different textures on the backs. Try for a medium size and then you can vary the sizes of the faux shells.

(four rows top to bottom)
steps to making shells

Shells

Begin by conditioning your clays, keeping the colors separate. You can use the white as your base color, or you can make an off-white shade by adding a little yellow and brown. Next, chop up your chosen shell colors. Chop, or use a grater, until the pieces are very fine, like coffee grounds or sand. It takes very little of the colored clay. Roll half of your base white into a ball, setting the rest aside. Use the ball to pick up some of the colored crumbs. Flatten the ball with your hand, a roller, or a pasta machine. Ball it up again, keeping the colors visible. Don't fold them into the middle. Fold the edges underneath, and stretch and smudge the colors. Add more of the white base color underneath if needed. Repeat this process until the colors are streaky and diffused, like watercolors.

Do the same process with the remaining base color, using either more or less of the same colors as before, or different colors for more variety. Then, cut or tear your clay into various sized pieces, and roll them into small balls, with the colors still visible. Flatten them into rounded or teardrop shaped pieces, about 1/4 inch thick. Make different sizes and shapes, some longer than others. Use the paintbrush to apply some talcum powder or cornstarch to the backs of the real seashells. The shells are your texture molds, and the powder is the release agent that keeps the clay from sticking. Press the clay onto the shell backs, and remove. Place onto your work surface, and poke a hole for stringing, if desired. Gently round the new faux shell outward so that it looks realistic.

shell sequence

When you have made as many as you like, use any scraps to make coordinating round beads, or twist and gently pull to form shells that are cone or horn shaped. This will also give a subtle stripe effect. Before I bake the faux shells, I like to pour a tiny amount of gold powder onto a jar lid (being very careful not to breath the powder), and I use one fingertip to pick up a very small amount, and gently smooth it onto the raised texture of the faux shells, to give a little shine to them without obscuring the colors.

(Important! If you want to gild the entire shell, you may wish to use the paintbrush, and also use a breathing mask because the brush makes the particles more airborne. This is especially the case with the FIMO bronze pulver, as it contains powdered aluminum, which can scar lungs when inhaled. The PearlEx powders contain mica instead of metal. The bronze pulvers are the most truly metallic looking, and are safe when used according to directions and with safety procedures.)

If the entire shell is gilded, seal the finish after baking with a coating of Flecto Varathane. If you are only using a small amount of the powders as a highlight, you will not need to coat the shells. If desired, use a pearl powder on the underside of the faux shells to simulate the nacre finish of many shells. Clean your hands after powder use.

Place the faux shells and beads onto a paper lined baking pan and bake according to package directions. Jump rings, or "O" rings, can be added after baking for ease in stringing, or you can knot the shells into place with your cord.

Coral

Mix some yellow and white into your red clay to make a faux branch coral. Very small amounts of black can also be added to simulate blood coral. Having some of each, rather than all the same, adds to the realistic effect. There are also white and black corals, if they fit your color scheme better. Coral is becoming more expensive and rare because of over harvesting, and now you can have the look without the cost or the guilt. Roll your blended clay into a pencil-shaped "snake," and continue to roll one end so that it has a thinner diameter. This gives you a variety in size as well.

Once you have the hang of it, also make some very small ones. Cut the snake into smaller pieces, ranging from 1/2 inch to an inch or so. Using the sandpaper or the crumpled aluminum foil, or both, lightly texture each piece. I gently press the paper or foil down onto the clay and roll the clay a few inches across the work surface. This puts the texture on all sides of the clay and leaves no fingerprints.

You can also do some without the texture, especially tiny branch coral pieces. You can then slice into one or both ends of the clay for 1/4 inch or so, forming a "Y" or "X" shape by opening the cut slightly, which simulates the branch effect. I usually trim one branch a little bit shorter than the other. Then, carefully pierce the center of the faux coral for your stringing hole, using the needle or toothpick. Insert first from one side, then the other, to make a neat hole and avoid "out-ies." Make quite a few, as they look best when strung in clusters, and remember to vary the size and coloration when stringing.

Place finished faux coral onto a paper-lined baking pan and bake according to directions. If a shiny "polished" finish is desired, give the baked pieces a light coating of Flecto Varathane, and allow to dry on waxed paper. Do not use the aerosol version of Varathane as the propellants are not clay compatible and your pieces will stay sticky.

Treasure Box

A wooden box painted blue was the basis for this little cache suitable for trinkets, treasures, or recipe cards. Baked polymer clay shells that match the ones on the light switch plate are glued into place on the top and sides of the box using white glue. A pearl or several are also glued into place. Line the box with an old map, a page from a travel magazine, or a piece of textured paper.

Buttons

These bright floral buttons might have been snapped up as trade goods in many a port of call. They were

available at one time from Quilts and Other Comforts, but only as a limited edition. It started as a 13-pound cane, and we are still using some of the remaining slices in upcoming projects. You can read the 13-pound cane saga in its entirety at my Web site (www.polyclay.com).

Perfume Bottles

Another variation for the same little perfume bottles has them covered with red and gold stamped clay, or faux cinnabar red, and even some of the 13-pound cane. Sometimes, having a lot of a cane can really encourage you to be adventuresome with what you do with it. These colorful little bottles make great gifts. You can also cover many old perfume bottle lids, as the hard plastic can take being baked in most cases. There is sometimes a blob of glue and a cardboard circle that comes out due to the heat of baking. This should be removed while hot.

Drawer Pulls

Painted wooden knobs are popped right into the oven along with the polymer shell in order to get a good fit to the curve. After baking, remove the shell, finish with Flecto Varathane if needed, and then glue into place on the knob.

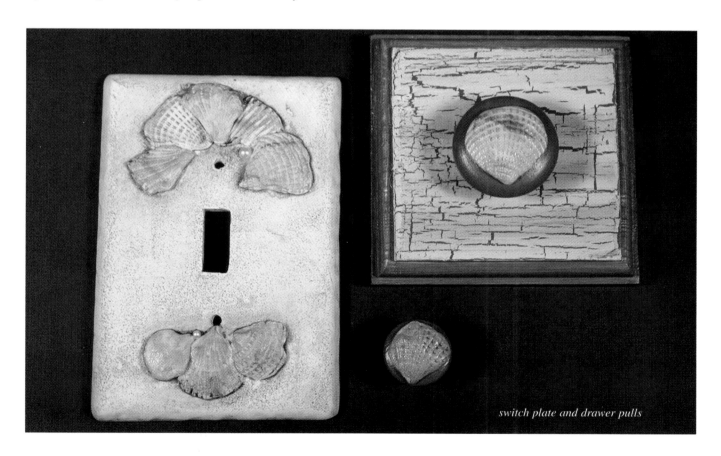

switch plate and drawer pulls

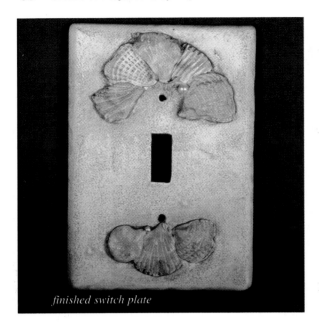

finished switch plate

sheet of clay, sandpaper and plate

trim, leave 1/4" allowance

back of plate

Switch Plate

Start with a clean PVC or metal switch plate, which can be found at any hardware store. Coat the face lightly with white glue and allow to become tacky or dry. Roll out a #4 setting sheet of clay in an ivory or beige color. Lay the switch plate face down on the sheet of clay.

cut out switch hole

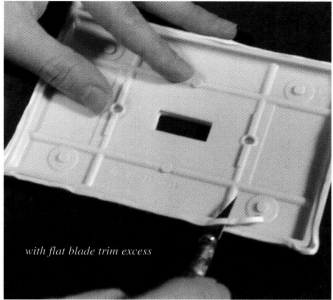

with flat blade trim excess

pierce screw holes

pierce again from front

Use a utility knife and trim excess clay, leaving a 1/4-inch margin around the entire plate. This is to accommodate the beveled edge. Use the blade right next to the center opening to cut out the little rectangle for the switch. Turn it over and smooth the clay downward all over the plate, easing the corners down. Make sure there are no bubbles—the glue helps a lot with this. Stroke the clay down over the edges just a bit.

Turn to the back again and try not to leave fingerprints in the front while you work. With the blade flat against the edge of the plate, trim away excess clay all around. Use a bead reamer or needle tool and poke through the screw holes so you can see them from the front. Then turn to the front and poke through the holes completely, making sure they are neat.

add texture

add to plate

press onto real shells for texture

peel away from shell

Impress the clay with texture at this point. I use a very gritty sandpaper, and press the sheet into the clay several times. After baking and staining, this will look a lot like sand.

Several seashells are made and pressed into place on the switch plate. These can be made to fit any color scheme. A little pearl powder on black clay makes a very convincing nacreous finish on the inside of one faux shell. A pearl bead is also glued into place. Bake the plate according to clay directions and it will not melt.

unstained switch plate

paint on stain, rub off

After cooling the baked piece, I stained it with my standard antiquing stain of Flecto Varathane, black acrylic paint and gold PearlEx powder. This is painted on with an old brush, scrubbed into the recessed areas, and then the surface is wiped clean with a T-shirt kept for the purpose, leaving only the recesses with paint.

After it is dry, the clay surface can be lightly sanded with an automotive finish sandpaper (2,000 grit) and water to remove any excess paint left on the surface. In this instance, the excess looked natural and was not removed.

Oriental

The opening of Japan to Western trade in the 1850s had a huge effect on the artistic world. Glowing lacquer colors, deep yet muted tones of cinnabar and jades, and indigo blues combined liberally with black and gold gilt to provide a rich palette. This seemed quite shocking next to European color schemes, where an abundance of pastels and shades of white and gold dominated. Even the Oriental artistic perspective was different, and asymmetry was quite a visual change from the formal traditions in European art. In addition, Japanese art encompassed the polar extremes of both exuberance of color and detail, and austere simplicity.

Of course, the Asian influences became wildly popular, adding to the opulence of the Edwardian Era and The Belle Epoque. The Eastern influence was seen in the bright colors of the Fauve Movement and in the work of Gustav Klimt, Edgar Degas, Vincent van Gogh, Mary Cassatt and many others.

The items in this section include:

- large and small beads
- tassel necklace
- drapery tie back
- filigree egg
- two wooden boxes
- switch and plug plates
- drawer pulls
- Noh mask pendant
- picture frame
- geisha box
- small box
- tray
- wall fan
- candlesticks
- doll

boxes and drawer pulls

Two Wooden Boxes

Cinnabar and Chinese red both are very strong, red colors, tending more towards yellow than blue. The acrylics used to paint the wooden items began with tomato red, black and a base of Flecto Varathane. Many coats were given to the wooden pieces to begin to simulate a lacquer finish. The top rim of the shorter box was painted black.

Premo gold and red clays were used to make the decorative parts of the lid handles. Rubber stamps provided texture and the pieces were pressed carefully into place on the lids, which were then baked for 25 minutes. There was a minor drop or two of glue that came out of the one wood lid during baking. I wiped it off while it was still hot and sanded the smear lightly with a fine sandpaper. Then I retouched the area with a bit of the original paint. It's always good to keep a lit-

tle of your paint batch when baking wood. I mix mine in recycled yogurt containers with plastic lids. They keep paint fresh for several days.

After baking, the clay was stained with a darker version of my standard stain. This stain is meant for colors, rather than faux ivory, and features the same Flecto Varathane, PearlEx gold powder, and black acrylic paint, but has much more black. This shows up against the darker background provided by the clay.

tall box

On the shorter of the two boxes, square and triangular tiles were glued into place using white glue. Once again I drew from my accumulation of tiles that are already baked and stained. I also make some specifically for these projects. Faux cinnabar squares and black-and-gold foil make a striking combination.

The taller box has round decorative pieces glued in place with small black tassels. These are easy to make or purchase and add to your work. The box also features a face made from my Noh mask mold, but is finished with touches of red and gold clay. The face itself is sanded and stained several times to give it the look of old, carved wood. While not completely traditional, this little face still has a very Oriental flavor.

Tray

This tray is made with a painted wooden tray and polymer clay tiles in the same way as the rose and ivory tray shown in the Victorian Roses section. The colors make a radical change in the overall effect, and this version has no transfer in the center. Instead, a sheet of gold and black clay, splashed liberally with gold leaf and gold powder stampings, was laid onto a piece of cardstock, and red pre-baked square tiles were placed in a pleasing design. The clay under each was cut with a utility knife and removed, then replaced with the red tile. The entire rectangle sheet was then trimmed and baked.

After baking, all the pieces for the tray were chosen and put together like a puzzle. This time, we put a piece of cardboard over the finished design, flipped it carefully, and were able to lay the entire thing out

*tray, boxes,
Noh mask necklace*

ental (close up)

tiles in piles

*Oriental beads, carved
& impressed pendants*

ready to be put back in after glue was added to the bottom of the tray. This made putting the pieces in much faster. The tray was then finished in the same way as the previous one.

Candlesticks

These candlesticks were painted red, and then red clay was impressed with an Oriental design and pressed carefully around the wood in places. After baking, it was stained and further adorned with a pendant (another square tile, with a hole in one corner and strung on gold thread with a large piece of faux coral).

Picture Frame

More of the square tiles were used to decorate the edge of the mat that frames a copper engraving. These were simply glued in place.

Noh Pendant

This was based on a picture of a Noh mask in the British Museum, and represents the Maiden character. I hand modeled the original pendant piece, then made an Elasticlay mold. Pulls from the mold often don't show the entire face, but are still useful for decorating, as in the box shown previously. A small, leather loop glued into place at the top of the head provides a carrier for the buna cord. Super glue works very well to bond leather to polymer.

Pins, Beads, Geisha Box

Cane work, used to build up images in a process like cloth applique, is used to decorate sheets of clay for these intricate images. No paints are used here, just colored clays that form the final pictures. The thin slices from as many as 40 different canes are used to create the details. If they are worked together carefully, it is hard to see the individual canes. The acrylic roller is very helpful in smoothing the top of these collages. A pasta roller can distort the image if care is not taken. One way to do this is to build the image on a #3 sheet of background clay, use thin slices, roll the image carefully with a roller or brayer, and then put it through the pasta roller at a #1 setting. This way, the collage is not much thicker than a #1 to start with, and does not spread as much. If needed, stretch the image slightly in the opposite direction to fix any spread. You can also make use of this as an effect—another "I meant to do that" instance. Images can be cut from the surrounding clay to make pins, or the sheets can be used to cover box lids or other forms.

When used to cover beads, the collages are built up over interior forms. Sometimes this is polymer clay, or wooden beads, sometimes larger forms. Even eggs can be turned into beads. The egg shown here is not made with cane work, but rather with gold Premo onlays. Other beads feature tiles that have been baked and then put into larger pieces of clay, which are then textured and pierced. After baking, the impressed pieces can be stained, or gold Premo can be sanded and buffed for some splendid mica effects. The use of Oriental motifs in rubber stamps is very popular, and these beads are a wonderful use for stamps. The necklace shown features red faux cinnabar impressed beads, cane beads, and faux coral beads, together with glass and metal beads as spacers to add interest and separation.

geisha box

Switch Plate and Plug Plate

Both of these were made using Premo and the matrix plates from some of my Ready Stamps. The switch plate is faux cinnabar, and the red clay was pressed into the matrix plate to texture it prior to being cut and placed onto the switch plate. After baking, it was stained with the darker Flecto and acrylic stain. The plug plate was made with gold Premo in the same way, but was baked and then sanded to remove the raised portions of the design. Progressively finer grades of sandpaper were used for this, with the last being wet/dry paper used underwater. This technique was also used to make decorative parts of the drawer pulls and some of the beads.

Drawer Pulls

Painted wooden pulls with red, gold or black polymer clay additions glued in place could be mixed or matched. A gold tassel is an excellent touch, whether hanging from a dresser, a door, the drapery, or the furniture. Beads and specially carved beads called netsuke and ojime were used in Oriental fashions at the ends of cords and fastenings, along with beautifully tied knots and ornate tassels.

Doll and Accessories

A simple cotton-knit cloth body, sewn, turned and stuffed, is used as a basis for this doll. Hands and a face mask are added, glued into place at the arms and head. The hands are individually cut and modeled, and the face is made using a mold, which was created in the same way as the Noh pendant mask, only smaller. Making and using a mold makes it easy to make limited editions of dolls. I can still tweak each one to make it an individual. This humble girl doll is finished with black cotton sewn hair and a bit of stain and paint on her face. The hands are also stained slightly to antique them. She is then dressed in cotton kimono made from scraps of vintage Japanese cloth. Her cotton knit body

switch plate faux cinnabar

makes her quite posable, and she kneels with a small tray and tea set, also made of polymer clay. Her geta (shoes) are made of polymer clay and a bit of shiny black string.

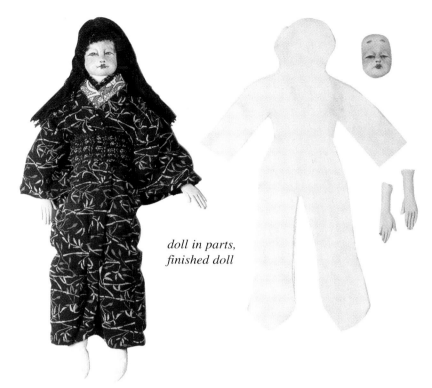

*doll in parts,
finished doll*

Japanese doll and accessories

Art Deco

The Oriental influence on art and fashion continued to evolve as European and American design elements incorporated all the elements of the times. Asymmetry and geometric precision met in a fusion of undulating curves and sharp angles; and Art Deco was born. Short for "Arts Decoratif," this style still held some flowing and natural elements of Art Nouveau, but in a more linear structure. The balance between restraint and freedom defines many artistic styles, and this was a time that gangsters and flappers flourished, Hollywood was just beginning its influence on style and there was access to luxury goods and materials side by side with poverty. Marble tile, black and silver lines, and curves in smooth progression help define this look, but are by no means the only expression of it. This was a time of unprecedented freedom in some ways—seen in the rise of popularity of black musicians and jazz music especially revered in Paris and New Orleans, and also seen in women's fashions.

The items in this section include:
- tray
- picture frame and sampler
- metal box
- masks
- switch plate
- drawer pulls
- dolls
- jacket
- earrings
- necklace
- pins
- wall hanging
- jacket

Art Deco

Dolls

For the first time in a great many centuries, women were not corseted into rigid curves. This lack of steel and whale-boned undergarments encouraged more movement and freedom in women, which resulted in loose clothing and very short skirts. For the first time women had visible legs! This caramel-colored doll, named Pearl, has the platinum blonde bobbed hair that was also a mark of freedom for women. The availability of women's cosmetics for daily use became more common, and short hair for women gained acceptance as well, although slowly. Madame, seen here with red hair and black feathers, is more conservative but still flamboyant in her own way, and both ladies would be at home in a speakeasy or gin joint.

Metal Box

A plain steel box was much improved by adding tile and a face made of polymer clay. Square sections over the corners camouflaged a messy solder seam. These were baked onto the lid, and then the face section was glued to a square mirror tile. Both were then affixed to the metal box.

Tray

Here's another wooden tray, finished with acrylic paints and polymer clay tiles, as were the Victorian rose tray and the Oriental tray. It is made using the very same techniques, but using only white, pearl white, black, silver, and gold. The mokume gane technique used in some tiles uses the metal foils to create circles in squares, and the alternating black and white patterns are structured yet playful. This tray would be stunning graced by a silver cocktail shaker and glasses.

madame in black

tray

Drawer Pulls, Plug Plate

The high contrast and geometric details on these items could be used to great effect today, with lush satin draperies or faux animal prints. Mixed with mirrors and black or blonde furniture, these pieces provide a stylish punctuation. The plug plate has a gold stamped star pattern across the top and bottom, with a gold-and-black area in the center of the plate divided from the stars by a jagged line of silver, a band of gold, and another strong linear pattern in black and gold.

drawer pulls and switch plate

Baubles, Bangles and Beads

Coco Chanel was responsible for the costume jewelry industry, making it very popular to wear multiple layers of beads and chains in long, skinny necklaces, multiple bracelets, bangles, and pins. Never before had the masses of ordinary women had access to such a profusion of personal adornment, and non-precious materials became the fashion rage. However, diamonds are always in style! The beads and pendants shown here would be fashionable worn by themselves or together, along with a jersey knit dress and a dozen bangle bracelets. The silver-and-black barrette would be great to help hold those marcelled waves in place.

beads, barrette, and pendants

masks

Masks

Masks have been popular throughout history, and these would fit right in at Mardi Gras. With black and silver details, these can actually be worn to a costume fete, but they would also be very striking as decorative elements hung on a wall. These would be particularly good to display with a collection of black vintage hats, or alongside a mirror, or two, or three…

Frame and Sampler

A simple black frame is brought to the Deco style with the addition of a black-and-silver stamped and impressed flourish that is first baked and then glued into place. Embellishments to frames can be done in the corners, along the top and bottom, or along the sides as desired. Though this one would be a great way to show off black-and-white photos, I've used it to showcase a sampler of triangular polymer clay pieces, mounted on red leather.

picture frame and sampler

Necklace and Earrings

A variety of different handmade beads are strung into this long necklace that would be perfect worn with a "little black dress" and a soft cloche hat. The beads are each separated by gold and black spacers that keep the long elegant line and prevent the larger beads from appearing clunky. A pendant bead at the bottom is another display of curves and angles, and is finished with a pair of jet-beaded dangles. The earrings have seed-beaded fringe reminiscent of a flapper's hemline.

Pins

These faces are also pulled from molds made from my own hand-built originals. They are more European than the Noh mask face. These are dressed in styles from the first part of the 1900s, with a soft cloche effect on one. These faces have been made into pins suitable for adorning a jacket or hatband. When not being worn, pins can be fastened to lengths of ribbon and used as room décor.

necklace and earrings

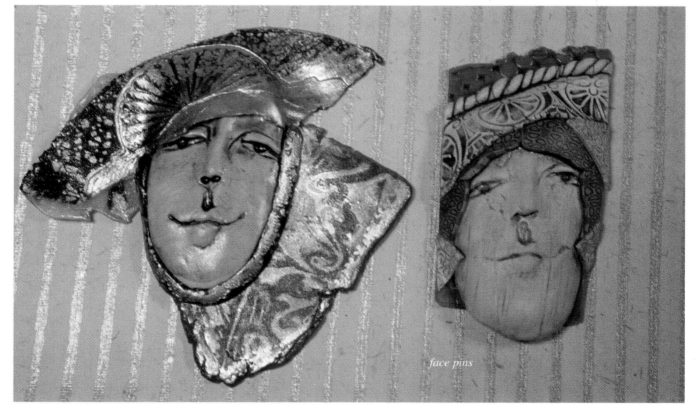

face pins

Jacket

Although this jacket is not strictly Deco, it is certainly decorated, and with a lot of black-and-white curvilinear forms and metallic accents. It began as a simple casual jacket of white with woven black lattices in the fabric. It was purchased by my mother, who found it too "busy." I, on the other hand, saw it as far too plain, and a natural coloring book. I filled in many of the squares using fabric paints and PearlEx powders. Then I sewed hundreds of buttons onto the squares. Many are vintage and made of metal and plastic, wood and bone. I have also used these classic beauties that I have collected to make molds that I use in making beads, buttons, and other items. There are a great many of these polymer clay buttons on this jacket as well. It's fun to hunt out the original and the reproduction and see the difference that color, size and finish can make. It's also a wonderful way to showcase my button collection.

button down jacket

face fan

Wall Fan

Another delicate-looking fan of epoxy resin and paper, made by Elaine Schaefer, is gussied up with the addition of a drawn face, polymer clay seashells, and feathers. She could be a dancer at the Follies! Polymer clay is a lightweight addition to hanging assemblages such as this.

Country Quilt

*Q*uilts made of fabric have always been a product of women's ability to utilize small individual components and leftovers. When pieced together, these segments form beauty from what might otherwise be wasted, and meld many different patterns and colors into an aesthetically pleasing whole. This can be done with polymer clay as well, and many quilt books can serve as inspiration when you're building canes, or combining them to form more intricate designs.

A quilt pattern known as "Grandmother's Fan" served as inspiration for this cane. Originally designed as a pin commissioned by *Quiltmaker* magazine for use as a promotional gift, it is like a quilt block in miniature. It was made by building five individual square canes into a rainbow of fabric-like floral prints. These were stacked to form long, rectangle canes, which were then each carefully cut to a fan-blade shape. Placed together to form a fan, the pieces were topped with a "lace" edging made of half circles of white and translucent clay. A background of indigo print was added to bring the cane back to square form.

When enough pieces had been cut to make the pins, I still had a bit left over, and liked it so much I made pieces for myself.

The items in this section include:

- ✂ tissue box
- ✂ trinket boxes
- ✂ whatnot drawers
- ✂ perfume bottles
- ✂ switch and plug plates
- ✂ drawer pulls
- ✂ beads and pieces
- ✂ candle holder
- ✂ picture frame
- ✂ light bulb vessel

country quilt

Wooden items such as the tissue box, the stack of whatnot drawers, and the papier-maché picture frame were first primed with several coats of Flecto Varathane and a deep mix of blue and purple acrylic paints, with a little added black. The results go beautifully with my pieces of cobalt glass. As shown in previous settings, perfume bottles and jars can be covered and made to belong together in your collection. Drawer knobs can be covered fully with sheets of clay, or decorated in the center with a single piece, as in these versions. The contrast between the blue wood and rosy cane slice shows off both. Though this is the same technique shown within the other settings, paint and clay colors make all the difference in the final result.

Grandmother's Fan cane

country quilt (close up)

Tissue Box

After the paint dried, white glue was used to affix baked slices of the Grandmother's Fan cane at and between the corners of the box, and clustered around the center opening. Slices from remainders of the peach-colored section were glued around the sides of the box. Spaces where the wood shows in between the peach colored clay slices give the effect of threaded ribbon.

Whatnot Drawers

"This and that, and whatnot" can all be tucked away in these little stacked drawers. They give added height to visual arrangements, and save space on a crowded dresser top. Impressed buttons in faux ivory are formed around the knobs, then removed and baked, and later glued in place. Coordinating faux ivory pieces anchor a fan cane slice at the top, and dot the side walls. These are all glued in place with white glue, as are the peach-colored cane patches on the fronts of the drawers.

Picture Frame

The painted papier-maché picture frame borders a beaded piece created by Amy Foltz. The fan cane slices glued at the corners of the frame complement the colors she has used in this exuberant stitchery. Amy also made the psanky egg shown on the dresser. This Ukranian egg-dying technique can provide great inspiration.

Quilt Box

Although the other boxes in this setting are made by covering metal or wooden boxes in the same manner as those shown previously, this one is a little different. The bottom of a wooden box was painted red, and a lace doily was glued to the top and sides of the box lid, using white glue, and draping the lace over the sides. Strings were tied around it while it dried, and then baked slices of several different quilt type canes were glued into place, making an arrangement that looks like piled patchwork of many kinds.

dresser with hanging necklaces and tiled mirror

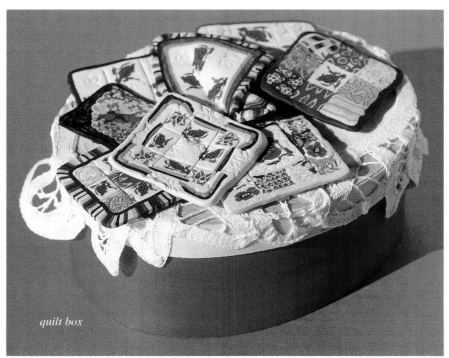

quilt box

care must be taken while covering the bulb with clay, and later when breaking the bulb after baking. This is done in a sealed bag, and the glass is shattered inside the vessel. Shards are poured out into a suitable container (I use an old laundry soap box). Then, using great caution and a skewer, any glass clinging to the side is loosened and removed. The lid is made from and old burned-out Christmas bulb, which was completely covered in clay and fitted to the mouth of the vessel. The bulb was left intact inside the clay covering after baking.

This sort of container is not waterproof and is best used in a decorative way. A note could be rolled up inside quite nicely, or small items hidden away. Unless you are quite thorough, there might still be some glass caught inside. This is not at all a project for children, but it was fun for the grownups at the Clay Day.

Switch Plate

Scraps of cane ends from the fan cane and a small amount of gold leaf were twisted to make a swirled and feathered looking sheet of clay. This was used to make the plates as shown in the previous section, and the switch plate was decorated with a star cut from a sheet made with fan cane slices, and placed at the top of the plate. The plug plate was stamped at the corners with a rubber stamp of my own design. After baking, both plates were given a coat of Flecto Varathane to protect the gold leaf and gold powder. It also serves to really make the colors pop out!

Candle

A blue candle in a heavy glass container looks good in this setting, but it looks even better with a ring of baked cane slices as ornamentation. The slices are glued to a strip of leather cut to fit around the container with 1/4 inch extra, where the ends are glued together to form a collar. A double spray of fan slices and a piece of faux ivory cover the seam and are glued in place. A blue ribbon ends in a bow at this point around the top of the candle.

Light Bulb Vessel

Marie Segal introduced me to the fun of covering light bulbs. After they've outlived their prime function, old bulbs can be carefully covered with sheets of warm, soft clay. Feet are added at the base, or a coil of clay can be added to provide stability. Great

light bulb vessel, and vessel with lid apart

Purple Patch

Purple is such a vibrant, regal color—it is no wonder that it has been the color of royalty and nobility for thousands of years. Even now, when everyone has access to colorful goods without restriction according to rank, the shades of purple from violet to wine are always immensely popular. Indigo and violet are at the end of the light spectrum, and these colors are said to soothe the spirit, and inspire creativity and spiritual growth. In this setting, some purple power is bestowed on items for the office.

Purple Patch

The items in this section include:
- desk set
- switch plate
- drawer pulls
- purple faerie puppet

*purple
faerie
puppet*

Puppet

It is always a good idea to have "on hand" an office wizard or faerie to keep things going smoothly. This one is a purple faerie puppet, made with a cotton body that was hand dyed and painted with glitter fabric paint. Her head and hands are polymer clay, with painted details. The head is formed around a blown eggshell, as was the mermaid's. With the hole at the small end of the egg enlarged, a cardboard tube can be inserted for the neck armature, and clay is formed around it and the egg together. A flange at the bottom of the neck is easily formed by stretching the clay end outward. After baking it is inserted into the glove/body at the neck opening. Then the flange is coated with white glue and the neck opening closed and attached to the neck flange. After this dries completely the hair is glued into place.

desk set

Desk Set

I bought a rather boring desk set for a dollar, knowing it could be fixed up with some paint and polymer clay. Shown here are the three pieces. The one on the far right shows the original decoration of the set. First the set was stripped of the pearl and gold emblems on the fronts. Everything then received several coats of purple paint.

The chrysanthemum canes were used in addition to other purple canes. Some were sliced and baked for collage type use. More thin slices were cut and applied to a rolled-out sheet of purple clay at a #1 Atlas setting. The decorated sheet-making technique is just like the one shown in the first section, but the arrangement of slices is different. To obtain a seemingly random but equal distribution, place five or six slices of one kind

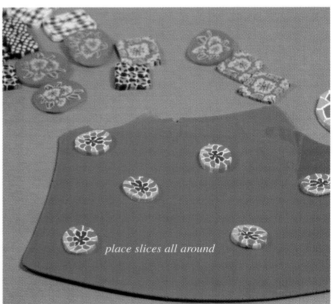

place slices all around

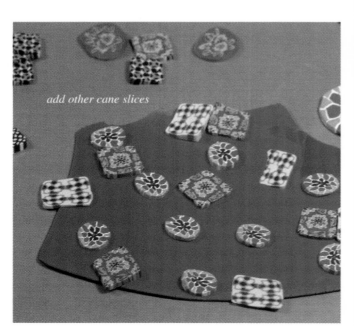

add other cane slices

continue to fill

roll flat

cut from the sheet

place raw clay on sides and bake

glue more baked slices

of cane so that they are in all areas of the purple sheet. Do the same with another kind of cane, and another. Fill in empty areas as you go and cut pieces of cane to fit as needed.

Roll the surface of the sheet using an acrylic rod or brayer, then run the sheet through the pasta roller and bring it to a #3 setting. Cut the sheets into smaller sections if need be to turn and run each section through the pasta roller from the other direction. This minimizes one-directional distortion as the canes spread evenly in all directions.

After painting, the desk set was decorated with cutouts of musical notes and stars. Any kind of cutters can be used, and the pieces can be baked separately or applied onto the container. You can even wrap around the edges, or cover the entire thing. Bake according to directions. Glue on additional pieces as desired. You can even take tiny scraps and apply them to make custom pushpins or thumbtacks for your memo board. Pens are a very popular item to cover, and the pen holders in this set give you a place to keep them.

Switch Plate

Use part of the sheet to cover switch or plug plates as shown in previous sections. The lace cane plates shown in the Victorian Roses section were made using this kind of sheet decorated with white, translucent and ivory instead of purple. You can also use it to cover box lids for those paper clips or other desk items, such as letter openers, magnifying-glass handles, etc.

Picture Frame

The cardstock frame was painted purple, and then spirals of glitter glue were added just as they were to the puppet's robe. After drying, baked cane slices, some cut to fit, were glued into place around the frame. You could decorate your computer monitor in the same way.

painted frame

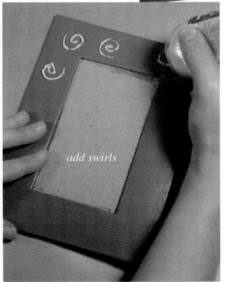

add swirls

drawer pulls

Drawer Pulls

This particular stamp is from Uptown Design Company (#G31084 Flowering Crest). It can also be seen used in the large pendant bead of the necklace in the antique ivory section. Here, it is used to make a drawer pull using purple clay and PearlEx powders in Interference Violet and Aztec Gold.

The rubber stamp is first lightly dusted using a ponce bag. A sheet of clay, rolled to a #3 Atlas thickness, is pressed into the rubber stamp. Make sure to include all portions evenly. The design should be bumpy all over the back of the sheet. Remove the sheet from the stamp and flatten carefully onto the work surface. Look at the open area of the cutter to center the design carefully, and use a circle cutter slightly larger than the top of the wooden drawer pull. Cut out a circle of impressed clay.

A wooden drawer pull, purchased at the hardware store, was first painted with the purple acrylic mix on the stem and underside of the knob. A coat of white glue was applied to the top face, and spread evenly all the way to the outside edge. The cut and impressed clay circle is then gently applied to the top, and the edges are carefully smoothed down and over the edge of the wood. Be sure not to flatten the image with undue pressure.

Using a fingertip or Q-Tip, apply gold powder to the outside portion of the design. Clean your finger using a baby wipe, or use another cotton swab. Apply the violet powder to the floral portion of the design element, leaving the flower center blank. Use a clean finger or swab to touch a bit of gold to the center of the flower. Bake according to directions and give the cooled piece a coat or two of Flecto Varathane to protect the powders.

An alternative is to use a knob that is painted fully, or a solid color to begin with. Elements can be cane slices or impressed shapes applied to the center of the knob, using white glue as before. The impressed element can be highlighted with PearlEx powders as shown, or stained after baking. You can choose to stop with the central element, or add more details. A twisted rope of gold clay softens the cut edge of the central motif. Added balls of gold clay, indented with the end of a paintbrush, circle the top of the drawer pull. Use the same techniques and drapery finials hardware instead of drawer pulls to further coordinate your window treatments.

powder rubber stamp

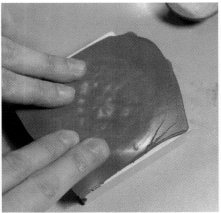

press clay into stamp

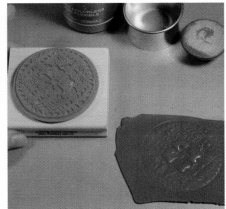

get a good image

cut out circle

add glue to pull

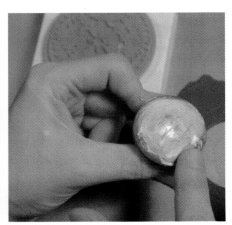

spread glue evenly

place clay onto pull

smooth down at edges

add gold powder at edge

add purple powder

rubber stamp and drawer pull

place in the center

add powder

twist a rope

add around the edges

add dots

indent with the brush end

drawer pulls

Techno Tribal

M y husband, Bryan, makes mosaic sculpture using the clay elements that I produce, others that he makes himself, and bits and pieces of collected treasures, including beads, dichroic glass, and vintage glass tiles. Patiently and with much thought to color, shape, and pattern, he chooses each element and affixes it into place over the form. Some of the larger pieces take many months to emblazon and encrust.

flower power flyer

The items in this section include:
- ✼ flower power flyer
- ✼ guitars
- ✼ Mosaic de Migraine
- ✼ sunlamp
- ✼ eggs
- ✼ masks
- ✼ clocks

flower power flyer (front view)

Flower Power Flyer

This piece had already had a long and useful life as a child's little red wagon. It was purchased at a yard sale, and Bryan cleaned it up and gave it a few coats of red Rustoleum™ paint. He then used a super glue to individually place thousands of tiles inside the bed of the wagon, and squares of clay with Victorian Floral transfers along the inner sides. More clay adorns the rim, the outside, even the wheels and the handle. It is a most beautiful and practical piece, which still rolls along quite freely.

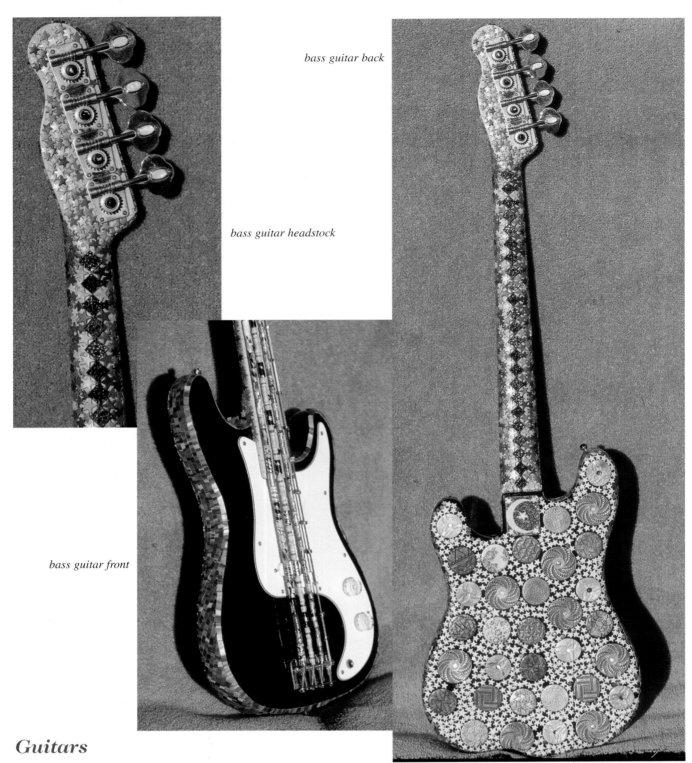

bass guitar back

bass guitar headstock

bass guitar front

Guitars

Bryan has done a series of musical instruments, giving new life to broken guitars as well as a violin and a banjo. These instruments no longer make much sound, but are still loud in their own way. The electric bass is a work in progress. The neck, sides, and back are covered in tiny pearly colored stars, many of which glow in the dark. The front face shows the beaded strings and the empty areas that will be covered next. Bryan usually finishes covering one surface area before moving on to the next. Finished areas must be padded and protected when turning to new portions.

The acoustic guitar has an extruded edging made with glittery glow-in-the-dark clay, which was baked and then applied. The strips of clay that layer the sides were cut using the linguini cutter attachment of the pasta roller (the big noodle is the linguini, the little one is a spaghetti) and the smaller strips were used to decorate the fret board.

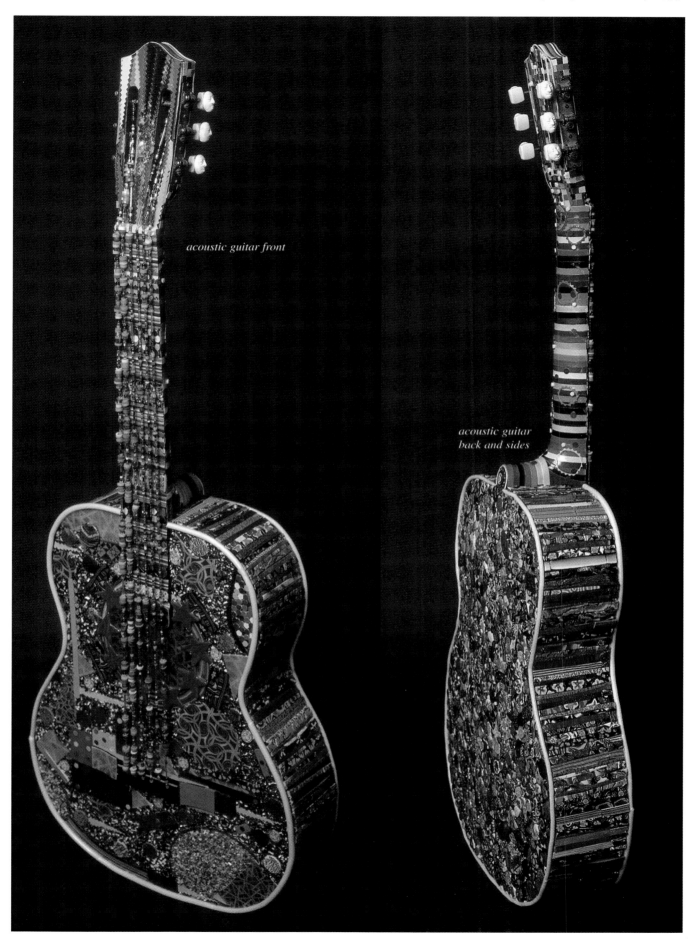

acoustic guitar front

*acoustic guitar
back and sides*

Mosaic de Migraine

Beginning life as a humble foam wig stand and a wooden plaque, this was our first mosaic collaboration. The head was first covered with thousands of cane slices. Because I was just learning how to cane, this piece has a lot of fairly simplistic slices, but they work well in such profusion! The face section is entirely in black-and-whites, and the rest is multi colored. After gluing all the pieces, Bryan and I threaded black glass beads onto craft pins and stuck them into the head between all of the slices. After 1,000 or so, we ran out of pins, and bought a few boxes more. All were stuck along with a black glass bead into the head, and still we saw bare spots, so we bought more pins. There are at least 3,000 pins sticking in this form. The head was affixed to the painted wooden plaque, and I added earrings with a sun and moon and a hand on each one. Several necklaces were looped around this display. It inspired us to use the term "techno-tribal" which we believe typifies our work pretty well, if someone is insisting on a label.

mosaic de migraine

Sunlamp

Sun canes and ribbons of striped clay were used to decorate this lamp. The minute bits of clay were made by running baked strips of clay at a #3 setting through the spaghetti cutter, and then further cutting the individual strands into pieces. All were arranged and glued into place around a lamp base. If you choose to cover and then bake a small lamp base, make sure you first remove all electrical cords. Lamps come in all shapes and sizes, and can be changed dramatically with polymer clay and a new shade. Also, lighting fixture hardware can be used to make some very interesting items into lamps. Consider covering the chandelier!

sunlamp

eggs

tasseled eggs

Eggs

Chicken, duck, goose, emu and ostrich eggs can be blown and covered with polymer clay. Used by themselves in a basket, hung from a branch on a ribbon, or strung up with a tassel, these offer a variety of festive possibilities. You can use them as drapery tiebacks or as Christmas ornaments on a fabulous fir tree or swag.

colorful masks

Masks

I was a participant in three Internet miniature mask "swaps," in which each artist sends in a required number of pieces plus a mailing label and postage to the swapmeister (the person running the swap). She divvies up the received items and each artist gets back one piece from every other artist. In this way I accumulated a terrific collection of little masks. I made more, and soon my display area was jumbled.

To do these tiny works of art justice, I chose to mount them all as a hanging collection. A sheet of high quality felted wool in a vibrant turquoise was cut to fit an existing piece of framed wood, and glued into place using a spray adhesive. This was done outside on a calm day with plenty of newspapers to protect the porch from overspray. The masks were arranged while the framed hanging was still laid flat on the floor, and each mask was glued into place using white glue on the backs and rims. I think of my Internet friends every time I see all these wonderful masks, and looking at it never fails to amaze me. Special thanks to all who have contributed to this collective work.

Formed over a porcelain mask and baked using sheets of decorated clay, these larger masks can be done in any color or style and look very showy hung on a wall. Use little nails at the ribbon knots by the temples to display them. Hang with pictures and mirrors, vintage hats and purses, or other decorative wall pieces.

The following artists contributed to the Internet mask swap collection: S. Helm, J. Valois, J. Braekel, J. Stotter, L. DeNio, E. Gibson, K. Schoubye, T. Biren, J. Van Donkelaar, C. Sherman, N. Draiman, P. Edmonds, S. Bailey, J. Skinner, M. Novak, Cynthia, Yoshi, V. LevRam, I. Helm, M. Therese, D. Parker, K. Guevarra, L. Tiffany-Cardwell, J. Galbraith, J. John, J. Winget, L. Van Horn, Eliana, P. Lillich, E. Berne, F. Maverick, T. Howell, V. Domanski, A. Gambino.

sun clock

moon clock

cane clock

Clocks

These clocks all had pieces of polymer glued into place. Though relatively few sun cane pieces are used for the day clock, the faces are charming enough to work on their own. This would be a delightful kitchen or sunroom clock, or it could be used in a child's bedroom. The cane clock has larger pieces at the hour stations, and a flood of pieces filling the center circle.

The hands are covered with glow-in-the-dark clay. The night clock shows opposing phases of the moon by flipping the slices of moon face cane. It is easy to glue pieces to plastic, wood or metal items of all sorts. Look around and see what you can use to create a polymer clay impression.

Sources

Abbadabba Productions, LLC
713 Blake Hill Road
New Hampton NH 03256
877-744-0002
babdu@lr.net
www.abbadabbavideo.com
instructional polymer clay videos

ACC Craft Markets/American Crafts
Council
72 Spring St.
New York NY 10012
888-313-5527
www.craftcouncil.org
magazine, organization, and shows

Accent Import/Export, Inc.
1501 Loveridge Rd Box 16 Unit 3C
Pittsburg CA 94565
800-989-2889
www.fimozone.com
*importers of FIMOsoft and FIMO clas-
sic, Magic Leaf Patterned leaf, blades,*

ACCI Association of Crafts and
Creative
Industries
Offinger Management Co.
P.O. Box 3388
Zanesville OH 43702
740-452-4541
acci.info@offinger.com
www.accicrafts.org

Aiko's Art Materials
3347 N. Clark
Chicago IL 60657
773-404-5600
*handmade Japanese papers, art   sup-
plies*

Amazon Drygoods
411 Brady Street
Davenport IA 52801
800-798-7979
info@amazondrygoods.com
www.victoriana.com/amazon
*vintage/ethnic patterns, shoes,
historical reproductions*

American Art Clay Co.
4717 W.16th St.
Indianapolis IN 46222
800-372-1600
www.amaco.com
clays, molds, books, tools, and more

American Science & Surplus
3605 Howard St.
Skokie IL 60076
847-934-0722
info@sciplus.com
www.sciplus.com
*interesting selection, tools, things to
cover*

Artistic Wire Ltd.
PO Box 1347
Elmhurst IL 60126
630-530-7567
www.artisticwire.com
colored wire, wirework tools and jigs

Bead & Button
P.O. Box 1612
Waukesha WI 53187
800-533-6644
customerservice@kalmbach.com
www.beadandbutton.com
magazine, Bead & Button trade show

Bead It!
152 S. Montezuma
Prescott AZ 86303
800-657-0304
mail@beadit.com
www.beadit.com
beads and findings

Beads Galore
2123 S. Priest St. 201
Tempe AZ 85282
800-424-9577
www.beadsgalore.com
beads, findings,supplies

Beedz
960 Yew St.
Bellingham WA 98226
877-733-8989
artaccents@shuksanonline.com
www.artaccents.net/beedz.html
tiny colored glass balls (no-holed)

Beyond Beadery
PO Box 460
Rollinsville CO 80474
303-258-9389
beyondbead@aol.com
http://members.aol.com/beyondbead
beads, findings, books, videos

Bobby Grieser
San Diego CA 92102
619-234-1089
bgrieser@earthlink.net
photography

Bradley's Plastic Bag Co.
9130 Firestone Blvd.
Downey CA 90241
800-621-7864
sales@bradleybag.com
www.bradleybag.com
bags and shipping supplies, gloves

CCHA Canadian Craft & Hobby
Assn.
#24 1410 40th Ave. NE
Calgary Alberta Canada T2E 6L1
403-291-0559
ccha@cadvision.com
www.cdncraft.org
organization

Center For Bead Research
Four Essex St.
Lake Placid NY 12946
518-523-1794
www.thebeadsite.com
bead info

CERF
P.O. Box 838
Montpelier VT 05601
802-229-2306
info@craftemergency.org
www.craftemergency.org
Craft Emergency Relief Fund

Clay Factory of Escondido
P.O. Box 460598
Escondido CA 92046
877-728-5739
clayfactoryinc@clayfactoryinc.com
www.clayfactoryinc.com
Premo, Cernit, Sculpey, cutters,tools, powders, more

Clay Quilt Junction 12467 61A
AvenueSurrey Canada V3X2E2
604-594-5188
ladydian@home.comwww.webhaven.c
om/crick/cqjboutique-/index.html
measuring & cutting tools, gridded work

Clearsnap, Inc
P.O. Box 98
Anacortes WA 98221
800-448-4862
contact@clearsnap.com
www.clearsnap.com
ColorBox inks, stamping supplies

Clotilde
B3000
Louisiana MO 63353
800-772-2891
www.clotilde.com
tools, books, threads, notions, more

Craftrends
741 Corporate Circle Suite A
Golden CO 80401
303-278-1010
dgardiner@primediasi.com
www.craftrends.com
magazine

Creative Paperclay
79 Daily Dr., Suite 101
Camarillo CA 93010
800-899-5952
www.paperclay.com
Paperclay modeling material

DAG Doll Artistisans Guild
607-432-4977
www.seeleys.com
organization, magazines

Daniel Smith
4130 First Ave. S.
Seattle WA 98134
800-426-6740
www.danielsmith.net
metal leaf, metal powders

Dick Blick
P.O. Box 1267
Galesburg IL 61402
800-447-8192
info@dickblick.com
www.dickblick.com
art supplies since 1911

Doll and Teddy Bear Expo
800-800-2327 ext. 227
bok@dollandteddyexpo.com
www.collectoreditions.com
Doll and Bear show

Doll Crafter Magazine
30595 Eight Mile
Livonia MI 48152
800-458-8237
www.scottpublications.com
magazines

DOLLS Magazine
1107 Broadway St. 1210 N.
New York NY 10010
800-588-1691
www.dollsmagazine.com
art and collectable dolls

Double Joy Beads
7119 E. Sahuaro Dr.
Scottsdale AZ 85254
800-497-3702
www.doublejoybeads.com
beads and findings

Dover Publications
31 E. 2nd St.
Mineola NY 11501
516-294-7000
www.doverpublications.com
Dover Books, Dover Pictorial Archive Series, clip art, and other incredible books

Dremel
4195 21st St.
Racine WI 53406
800-437-3635
www.dremel.com
tools, including MotoTool

Eastern Findings
19 West 34th Street
New York NY
800-332-6640
efcsales@easternfindings.com
www.easternfindings.com
findings

Eberhard Faber GmbH
Postfach 1120
Neumarkt Germany 92302
09181/43 0-0
manufacturer art supplies, FIMO

Elaine Schaefer
mselainey@peoplepc.com
contact through Sarajane Helm
paper and resin fans; wall art

Elsie's Exquisiques
722 Lenox Ave.
Riverside CA 92504
800-742-SILK
karensnyder92504@yahoo.com
www.elsiesgarden.com
braid, silk and vintage ribbons, trims, supplies, silk roses

Embellishment
Quilts, Inc., 7660 Woodway,
Suite 550
Houston TX 77063
713-781-6864
shows@quilts.com
www.quilts.com
Embellishment trade show, quilt & sewing shows

Factory Direct Craft Supplies
P.O. Box 16
Franklin OH 45005
800-252-5223
Krafts2u@aol.com
www.crafts2urdoor.com
supplies, stamps, stencils, papermache

Fancifuls Inc.
1070 Leonard Road
Marathon NY 13803
607-849-6870
http://www.fancifulsinc.com
brass charms

Fantastic Fantasies
P.O. Box 3281
Allentown PA 18106
610-481-9306
fanfandolls@compuserve.com
www.fantasticfantasies.net
gallery of contemporary doll art

Fiber Studio Press
20205 144th Ave. NE
Woodenville WA 98072
800-426-3126
info@patchwork.com
www.patchwork.com
magazines

Fiberarts Magazine
Nine Press, 50 College St.
Asheville NC 28801
704-253-0467
editor@fiberartsmagazine.com
www.larkbooks.com
magazine

Fire Mountain Gems
28195 Redwood Hwy., Dept. 8418
Cave Junction OR 97523
800-355-2137
catalog@firemtn.com
www.firemountaingems.com
beads, supplies, findings, more

Flax Art and Design
240 Valley Drive
Brisbane CA 94005
888-352-9278
www.flaxart.com
art supplies, gifts

Gameplan Artranch
2233 McKinley Ave.
Berkley CA 94703
510-549-0993
www.gameplan@earthlink.net
instructional videos

Gold's Artworks, Inc.
2100 Pine St.
Lumberton NC 28358
800-356-2306
www.goldsartworks.20m.com
metal leaf, papermaking supplies

HIA Hobby Industry Assn.
P.O. Box 348
Elmwood Park NJ 07407
201-794-1133
hia@ix.netcom.com
www.hobby.org
Hobby and Craft tradeshow

HR Meininger
499 Broadway
Denver CO 80203
800-950-2787
webmastr@meininger.com
www.meininger.com
*art supplies from around the world
since 1880*

I.B. Moore
648 Laco Drive
Lexington KY 40511
859-255-5501
www.ibmoore.com
buna cord, rubber O rings

Ichiyo Art Center, Inc.
432 East Paces Ferry Rd.
Atlanta GA 30305
800-535-2263
www.ichiyoart.com
washi paper, rubber stamps

INM Crystal
7375 Tillman Dr
Lake Worth FL 33467
561-964-2234
inmcrystal@yahoo.com
www.inmcrystal.com
*crystal beads, pendants, prisms, and
collectables*

Intergalactic Bead Shows
P.O. Box 2293
Asheville NC 28802
888-729-6904
www.beadshows.com
bead trade shows

Interweave Press
201 E. Fourth St.
Loveland CO 80537
800-645-3675
DonnaM@Interweave.com
www.interweave.com
magazines

J&J Promotions, L.L.C.
8490 W. Colfax Ave. CS-27 Box 334
Lakewood CO 80215
303-232-7147
www.beadshow.com
Bead Renaissance Shows

Jaquard-Rupert Gibbon & Spider, Inc
P.O. Box 425
Healdsburg CA 95448
800-442-0455
www.jaquardproducts.com
*PearlEx Powders, dyes and fabric
paints*

JASI
P.O. Box 263
Hygiene CO 80533
JASI@polyclay.com
www.polyclay.com/jasi.htm
Judith Skinner's Cane Slicer

Jewelry Crafts Magazine
4880 Market St.
Ventura CA 93003
800-784-5709
jewelrycrafts@pcspublink.com
www.jewelrycrafts.com
magazine

King Tool Inc.
5350 Love Lane
Bozeman MT 59718
800-587-9445
www.king-tool.com
pin vise drills, tools

Krause Publications
700 E. State St.
Iola WI 54990
800-258-0929
www.krause.com
books and magazines

La Cuisine
323 Cameron St.
Alexandria VA 22314
800-521-1176
lacuisine@worldnet.att.net
www.lacuisineus.com
*handmade, Japanese, and commercial
canape/cookie cutters, molds, tools*

Lapidary Journal
60 Chestnut Ave, Ste. 201
Devon PA 19333
800-676-4336
lapidaryjournal@primediasi.com
www.lapidaryjournal.com
magazine

Lavender Lane
7337 Roseville Road Suite #1
Sacramento CA 95842
888-593-4400
healthychoices@lavenderlane.com
www.lavenderlane.com
bottles and jars, containers, oils

Main Street Mat Co.
245 Main St.
Longmont CO 80501
303-776-4840
msmco1@qwest.net
www.mainstreetmat.com
industrial floor mats, many sizes and colors

MIAA Miniatures Industry Association
of America
P.O. Box 3388
Zanesville OH 43702
740-452-4541
miaa.info@offinger.com
www.miaa.com
organization

Micro Mark
340 Snyder Ave.
Berkeley Heights NJ 07922
800-225-1066
www.micromark.com
earth pigments, carving and   modeling

NAME (National Association of
Miniature Enthusiasts)
P.O. Box 69
Carmel IN 46082
317-571-8094
name@miniatures.org
www.miniatures.org
organization

National Polymer Clay Guild
PMB 345 1350 Beverly Rd., 115
McClean VA 22101
www.npcg.org
polymer clay user's organization

NIADA
National Institute of American Doll
Artists
www.naida.org
doll artists organization

Ornament Magazine
P.O. Box 2349
San Marcos CA 92079
800-888-8950
ornamentmagazine.com
magazine

Ornamental Resources
1427 Miner St. Box 3010
Idaho Springs CO 80452
800-876-6762
www.ornabead.com
stones, charms, beads, findings, supplies, more

OTT-LITE
1214 W. Cass St.
Tampa FL 33606
800-842-8848
www.ott-lite.com
true color lighting

Paragon Industries, Inc.
2011 South Town East Blvd.
Mesquite TX 75149
800-876-4328
paragonind@worldnet.att.net
www.paragonweb.com
Art Clay Silver, Gold, kilns

Perfect Touch
24 Artesia
Conroe TX 77304
409-756-1942
www.perfect-touch.com
artist tools

Polyform Products
1901 Estes Ave.
Elk Grove Village IL 60007
847-427-0020
www.sculpey.com
manufacturer of Sculpey, Premo clays

Prairie Craft Co.
P.O. Box 209
Florissant CO 80816
800-779-0615
vernon@pcisys.com
www.prairiecraft.com
clay supplies, tools

Ready Stamps
10405 San Diego Mission Road,
Ste. 103
San Diego CA 92108
619-282-8790
www.readystamps.com
custom rubber stamps

Rings & Things
P.O. Box 450
Spokane WA 99210
800-366-2156
www.rings-things.com
wholesale jewelry findings and beads

Rio Grande
7500 Bluewater Road NW
Albuquerque NM 87121
800-545-6566
bluegem@riogrande.com
www.riogrande.com
beads, gems, findings, supplies, tools

Rishashay
Box 8271
Missoula MT 59807
800-517-3311
inquire@rishashay.com
www.rishashay.com
Bali silver and gold plate beads, caps,findings, chain

Sarajane's
P.O. Box 263
Hygiene CO 80533-0263
sarajane@polyclay.com
www.polyclay.com
beads, buttons, wearable art, dolls, sculpture and more

SCD Society of Craft Designers
P.O. Box 3388
Zanesville OH 43702
740-452-4541
scd@offinger.com
www.craftdesigners.org
organization

Seeley's Doll Supplies
118 Commerce Rd.
Oneonta NY 13820
800 433-1191
www.seeleys.com
doll making supplies, magazines

Shipwreck Beads
2500 Mottman Rd. SW Dept. B1
Olympia WA 98512
800-950-4232
www.shipwreck-beads.com
beads and findings, tools and more

Soft Flex
P.O. Box 80
Sonoma CA 95476
707-938-3539
sfwtm@softflextm.com
www.softflextm.com
Softflex Wire, Artistic Wire

Somerset Studio
22992 Mill Creek, Ste. B
Laguna Hills CA 92653
877-STAMPER
www.somersetstudio.com
*stamping, paper/book arts magazine,
also "Belle Armoire" magazine for
wearable art*

Speedball Art Products
P.O. Box 5157
Statesville NC 28687
800-898-7224
www.speedballart.com
carving tools and more

Stampers
10501 8th Ave. N.E. #107
Seattle WA 98125
206-367-2371
marya@uswest.net
www.magicalfaerieland.com
*Faerie Glass, Faerie Dust --colored
ground glass, pearlescent powders*

Tandy Leather
P.O. Box 791
Fort Worth TX 76101
888-890-1611
www.tandyleather.com
leather, cords, tools, metal stamps

The Artist's Alternative
10 Sims Road,.
W. Hartford CT 06117
800-927-8258
www.mypaint.com
discount art supplies

The Crafts Report
300 Water St.
Wilmington DE 19801
www.craftsreport.com
magazine, show listings and reviews

The Flecto Co., Inc
1000 45th St.
Oakland CA 94608
800-635-3286
www.flecto.com
*Flecto Varathane Diamond Wood
Finish (interior)*

The Whole Bead Show
P.O. Box 1100
Nevada City CA 95959
800-292-2977
info@wholebead.com
www.wholebead.com
The Whole Bead Show

Thomas Scientific
I-295 Box 99
Swedesboro NJ 08085
800-345-2100
www.thomasscientific.com
tissue blades

Threads Magazine
63 S. Main St.
Newtown CT 06470
800-888-8286
www.taunton.com
magazine

TSI, Inc.
101 Nickerson St.
Seattle WA 98109
800-426-9984
tsiaid@aol.com
www.tsijeweltools.com
*jewelry supplies, polymer clay,
jewelry*

Uptown Design Company
10 Caledonia Summit
Browns Point WA 98422
800-888-3212
www.uptowndesign.com
stamps, powders, inks

US Art Quest Inc.
7800 Ann Arbor Rd.
Grass Lake MI
MI 49240
800-200-7848
www.usartquest.com
Perfect fx mica flakes, granules

WDP Studio
1757 Killarney Dr.
Holt MI 48842
517-699-7788
wdpstudio@dellnet.com
http://wdpstudio.safeshopper.com
*polytool bead rollers, PearlEx,
Powdered Pearls, Perfect FX, chain,
wire, buna*

Wee Folks Creations
18476 Natchez Ave.
Prior Lake MN 55372
612-447-3828
weefolk@weefolk.com
www.weefolk.com
polymer clay, molds, classes, videos

Williams-Sonoma
P.O. Box 7456
San Francisco CA 94120
800-541-2233
www.williams-sonoma.com
(kitchen) tools, things to cover

ZigZag Polymer Clay Supplies
15 Pascoe Ave.
St. Albans Christchurch,
New Zealand 8001
+64-3-385-4436
petra@zigzag.co.nz
www.zigzag.co.nz
polymer clay, supplies, tools

About The Author:

Sarajane Helm has been making, collecting, and arranging things all her life. She was trained as a theatrical designer and illustrator. Since 1978 she has made and sold dolls and wearable art in many forms, using her skills with fabric and fibers, polymer clay, and paper media.

She creates and sells her polymer clay art, and her work is seen in the form of magazine articles, textile and rubber stamp designs, paper dolls and other graphics. She teaches the occasional class, and has at least 10 projects going at any one time, including learning computer skills to build better Web pages.

With her husband, Bryan, who is also a musician, she collaborates on larger polymer sculpture. Creativity is an important part of their family life. They live in Colorado area with their sons and everybody gets involved in clay fun. Sarajane is also a member of local polymer clay guilds and the National Polymer Clay Guild.

Visit www.polyclay.com to find out more.

About The Photographer:

Bob Grieser has been a photojournalist for almost 30 years, beginning with his career at the Washington Star and later the Los Angeles Times. He focused on the White House, heads of state, politics and disasters, the Olympics and rock-and-roll, as well as daily journalism and the lifestyles of the rich and famous.

Bob's heart is tied to the sea, and he has devotedly covered the yachting world for more than 20 years with his work appearing regularly in national and international publications. In 1989, Harry Abrams Books published his book *Chesapeake*, a 232-page collection of black-and-white photographs of the environs of Chesapeake Bay, with a foreword by James A. Michner.

Bob was one of six photographers selected to illustrate the official record of the *America's Cup* published by Graphic Inc. in 1992, and one of three for the 1995 *America's Cup Book* published by Tehabi Books.

He and his wife, Georgia, live in San Diego with their two golden retrievers.